Age of Freedom

Women at the Crossroads of Career and Change

Janet A. Gregory and Janice Hulse

Independently Published
Printed by Amazon.com, Inc.

www.kdp.amazon.com

ISBN-13: 9798528485355

Dedicated to

all the amazing women

who stay true to themselves,

and the courageous, giving, and lifelong learners.

Contents

Acknowledgements

Ed Gregory – patience and encouragement
Kirk Hulse – patience and encouragement

Thank you for generous assistance in manuscript review:

- Cynthia Barlow – early reader and review
- Susan Castoro Brooks – early reader
- Nancy Frohman – early reader
- Karyn Holl – early reader
- Linda Kitchens – early reader
- Pat McCarthy – early reader
- Gina Schaefers – early reader
- Megan Sheldon – early reader and review
- Janet Silverman – early review of select chapters
- Juanita Timmons – early reader
- Marta Vickers Anderson – early reader
- Susie Williams – early reader

Thank you for kindly sharing personal stories:

- Ann Burton
- Leslie Canning
- Maureen Fisher
- Mary Gospe
- Nina Jobe
- Eve Joy
- Annmarie Neal
- Juanita Timmons
- Kimmy B. Tyson
- Donna Weber

Thank you for sharing thoughts and perspectives:

- *Semi-anonymous:* Susan H, Roberta P, and Dana Y
- *Anonymous:* 650+ professional women that responded to our survey

Thank you for helping make this book possible:

- Megan Quinn, copywriting and editing
- Mitch Hulse, content and website consulting
- Theresa Lambert, book marketing ideas
- Dorothy F. Anderson, contributed her research on a similar topic from 1985-1987
- Joyce Anderson, permission to reprint a handmade, hand-painted card from 1985
- David James, cover finalization

We are forever grateful for the wealth of resources, information, and images available online. Here are a few of our favorite resources:

- Dictionary.com
- Dreamstime.com
- Merriam-Webster.com
- Search engines: Google, Bing
- TheNounProject.com
- VectorStock.com
- Wikipedia.com

Preface

Age of Freedom

Women in their professional careers always look forward. What's next? What lies ahead? Where will the path lead? Dynamic, professional women encounter many crossroads that are intermingled with career and personal choices. We are faced with different roads to follow, sometimes not knowing where that path will lead. In this age of freedom, the possibilities are remarkable.

This book explores how women embrace the age of freedom whether they are working in the eye of the storm, embracing a new career, reinventing themselves working on their own terms, or expecting the unexpected.

The book is filled with stories, ideas and learnings. All are spoken from the heart. They are entertaining, dramatic, humble, happy, or sad; yet all are perceptive. The insights are just as unique as the 650+ professional women from around the world who contributed them.

It is about the freedom exercised in choices we make within our relationship to work. Freedom to leave some things behind and embrace what's ahead. Freedom to let surprises unfold – delightful or unpleasant.

This is why we, Janet and Janice, wrote this book.

We were both at our own crossroads of change. We wanted to hear and learn from other professional women like ourselves. We began to look at the work-world through a different lens. We wanted to validate our thinking through the voices of other women and their experience.

Gleefully, we realize that retirement belongs at the back of the shelf, collecting dust like an old set of encyclopedias.

This book is unlike any other. It is not about retirement, career change or winding down. It's about the intersections professional women encounter and the choices we make. Most importantly, it's about being true to oneself.

Chapter 1

Free to Choose

Professional women are always growing, learning, and striving in some capacity. If we aren't, we would be shrinking, withering, or unmotivated – and we don't want to go there.

The age of freedom transcends time and space. Space has three dimensions that describe volume: width, breadth, and height. Time is the fourth dimension, a scaler. Similarly, the age of freedom has three dimensions: the width of our evolving and changing relationship with the work-world, the breadth of our activities, and the height of our sense of purpose. Time is also the fourth dimension. We get to choose what we do and when we want to do it.

Professional women are multi-dimensional.

There is an image that has circulated for years and continues to circulate regularly. It is the image of a woman with multiple arms juggling many different things. The items being juggled vary according to the topic being addressed, but there are always many diverse items adeptly held in the air surrounding the woman's head.

This is who we are. This is us. We have our hands and our minds involved in a wide variety of things at any given time. Some of those things are cerebral, complex, and require significant intellectual energy. Some are practical, real-world, and just need to be done. We juggle all sort of things that are work-related or family matters, public or private, job or leisure; the list can seem endless.

We juggle all of these choices because that's what we do. It doesn't mean it's easy, unrestricted, or tranquil. But as professional women we do have a large margin of choice and freedom to juggle what we do. Yes, freedom. The word freedom seems to best describe it. We are living in an age of freedom.

We fulfill a variety of roles: employee, employer, provider, caregiver, spouse, sibling, partner, parent, grandparent, and more.

We move through several lifecycle stages as we grow:

- Coming of age – adolescence, go-go, courtship, prime.
- Nurturing – reproducing, adopting, raising children or grandchildren, caregiving.

- Transforming — refining, redefining, reinventing, adventuring.
- Maturing — decompressing, stabilizing, unwinding, sustaining.

We move through these lifecycle stages not just once, but many times in our lives. If spouse or life-partner relationships change, your life may cycle back through nurturing and transforming. For some women, becoming a grandparent cycles them back into nurturing.

Independently, our work life also moves through these stages. Our work life can cycle through all four of the stages as we change company, career field, or leadership level.

Coming of age in the work-world begins as an individual contributor, apprentice, junior partner, or someone just starting out. It is a time of exploration, assessment, and skill acquisition.

Nurturing oneself and others in the work environment evolves from working in or on a team to supervising people or processes. Nurture is very fulfilling as we become established in an industry or a functional role and work effectively with others.

Transforming is when we commit to our chosen field. We are in a mode of deep learning and leading. This is a time when we, as professionals, take on greater responsibility and accountability. It is also a time when we may adventure into new roles. Some women take on new levels of management, executive leadership, or business ownership. Others dedicate themselves to excellence, innovation, and governance in their individual contribution.

5

Maturing in our careers is a time of stability, sharing expertise, and mentoring. This is when we may add new roles as advisor, coach, or board member to our work relationships.

We sought out women that are established in their careers and had progressed beyond 'coming of age' into nurturing, transforming, or maturing. We were interested in connecting with women who had achieved a certain "something" in their work life; women who had moved beyond the starting out phase.

Being in-stride or having achieved a level of experience in a career provides a solid foundation from which other opportunities can arise.

With a strong career foundation, women establish their core values which support and guide them. This good foundation is central to who we are, holding us accountable to ourselves, others, decisions we make, and things we do. A solid career foundation gives us options and choices that we might not otherwise have.

We circulated a survey, then a follow-up survey, and connected with professional women for their insight, learning, and stories.

The women we connected with identify themselves as being in one of three work-related categories:

- Working full-time, intensely in the midst of their career and fully engaged. These women are in the thick of it.

- Working but not necessarily full-time. These women are working on their own terms which includes moving in and out of the work-world or even relaxing their work relationship in some way.
- Women who have stepped away from full- or part-time work, so they are out of the paid work world.

Why read *Age of Freedom*?

It's not a one-size-fits-all world or even one-size-fits-most. Through surveys and interviews, we saw common characteristics from a wide variety of professionals. We also saw common leadership skills expressed at every leadership level from individual contributor to business owner. The common denominator is the ability to choose.

COVID-19 has changed some of the choices. But, if it wasn't a global pandemic, there would be some other catalyst for change. Destabilizing events occur all the time; they change the way we live and work. Just look over your shoulder at some of the things that have dramatically changed our lives: globalization, technology, the financial crisis of 2008-09 that impacted world economies, the September 11 attacks on the World Trade Center in New York City, and unforeseeable natural disasters.

Globalization and technology are not events but more driving factors in everything from economics to culture and to politics. It affects trade, migration and movement of people, as well as capital and investment opportunities. Financial crises, 9/11, and natural disasters are events with high impact in a short period of time that have long reaching effect, like an explosion with the resulting shock waves.

We won't really know the impact of the COVID-19 pandemic until years ahead when we can look over our shoulder. The global pandemic appears to be a combination of both an event and a driving factor. As an event, it can be measured by the day – when restrictions were put in place, a friend or loved one was lost, a vaccination received, or a business was shuttered. The pandemic is also a driving force, forever changing connections with healthcare, live performances, large gatherings, government, or other cultures through travel.

We were fascinated with how women change their relationship with work, especially as they advance in their careers or pivot to a completely different direction in the work world. As we dug deeper into this topic, we were surprised to find so little literature dedicated to it.

There are numerous support mechanisms for women launching their careers or helping professional growth mid-stride. Educational institutions offer degrees and certifications. Companies and organizations provide internships, training, mentors, and apprenticeships. Industries present support groups, networks, conferences. But where are the support mechanisms for professional women at or nearing their top professional achievement?

Generally, we are forced to discover this on our own. It is as if we are alone in our questioning about what's next as we explore our changing relationship with the work-world. As professional women, we plow ahead. We make decisions and move forward with confidence, even if a bit blindly. As professionals, we are not afraid to tackle tough issues or venture into the unknown. More than not, that's been a hallmark of our successful career.

Yes, there is an expansive amount of literature dedicated to self-improvement, self-help, development, and inspiration; we have read many.

Age of Freedom is none of the above. It is designed specifically for you: the professional woman at or nearing her top professional achievement and who is at a crossroads of change. A woman interested in understanding how her relationship with work may change in time because of professional or personal choices.

Age of Freedom lets you:

- ✓ Explore new relationships with the work-world from in-depth evaluations by women who are living those new relationships.
- ✓ Recognize some of the choices that are possible.
- ✓ Connect through stories from incredible professional women who speak their mind and share their voices. Some may have a very different viewpoint than you do.
- ✓ Discover work-life balance and wellness from innovative vantage points.
- ✓ Acknowledge how high-impact catalysts of change exert influence on our personal, professional, and travel lives.

We learned that a strong career foundation affords women a certain freedom and independence. Career women have the ability to choose, transform, or invent in good times and bad. In good times, the sky is the limit. In bad times, their strong foundation keeps them grounded.

The areas of distinction that rise to the surface for many of the women who shared their stories and insights are:

- Having the freedom of choice.
- Changing direction, transforming, and "unthinking" thoughts.
- Opening many options that add to life.
- Exercising the capacity to act.
- Expressing personal independence, shedding the shackles, removing restrictions, saying "yes" or "no".
- Being inventive and adventuresome.

Our choices are many. We are women who are constantly evolving, no matter what lifecycle or work-cycle stage we are in at a particular moment in time.

Nothing makes me more nervous
than people who say, "It can't happen here."
anything can happen anywhere
given the circumstances.
Margaret Atwood, 2015 lecture at West Point
Canadian novelist, teacher, environmentalist, inventor

Chapter 2

Voices of the Age of Freedom

Women from around the globe shared their thoughts with us through surveys, interviews, and inquiries. The responses are open, honest, revealing, and sometimes raw.

We share comments from these women in their own words. You will find their words in quotes or indented-with-distinction, emphasized by ∞ an infinity loop. At times we reveal their names and individual stories, while some quotes stand anonymously alone. Others are combined with like-thinking women so you can read their collective thoughts.

We listened carefully and learned from the women with whom we connected. The original concept for the book changed radically. We initially thought to write a book about professional women retiring. The research dramatically altered that concept into a book for and about women changing their relationship with the work-world.

In the midst of writing and analysis, the global COVID-19 pandemic hit, altering the concept further.

In this chapter we are pleased to briefly introduce you to the 650 women, aged 40 to 80, who shared their stories with us. We give you a quick snapshot of who they are. If you want more detail, numbers, and charts spend some time reviewing *Appendix 1: Strength of the Voices.*

Relationship to the work-world

Very early in any conversation with a professional woman, we describe our relationship with the work-world. In our own words, we describe ourselves within one of three general categories.

- Working full-time, in the **thick-of-it** and fully engaged.

- Working on **my-own-terms** but not necessarily full-time, which can include moving in and out of the work-world or even relaxing the work relationship in some way.
- No longer working with an income motive and are **out-of-the-paid-work-world.**

Nearly half of the women responding to our survey are working full-time, intensely involved in their careers, and in the thick-of-it. They are working, enjoying it, and not ready to change their relationship with the work-world.

A quarter have redefined their relationship with work; they are engaged and working but not necessarily full-time. Many have started their own business, consult, or coach. Others work part-time. All of them juggle multiple roles and have designed their own unique relationship with the work-world to better suit themselves. They are working on my-own-terms.

Relationship to Work-World

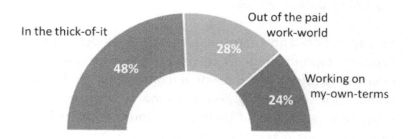

A bit more than a quarter are out-of-the-paid-work-world and have reinvented themselves. The antiquated word "retirement" comes to mind, but as we learned that term does not describe where they are in their life's work. The women in this group are working, the difference is that there is no income associated with the work they do. Some women in this category also enjoy other pursuits that they consider more "playtime" than work.

If the same women answer the survey today, the numbers will look different. Many factors contribute to women changing their relationship with the work-world: family, health, business, personal choice, and unexpected events, like the COVID-19 pandemic. Many women move back and forth, changing their relationship to the work-world by choice or necessity.

Our relationship with the work-world also contains other details, such as our leadership role, functional area of responsibility, industry or market segment.

For three-quarters of the women responding to our survey, these details reflect where they _are_, which is in the thick-of-it and working on my-own-terms. For the remaining quarter who have stepped out-of-the-paid-work-world, it's a combination of _are or were_ depending on the focus of their current or past activities.

Survey respondents represent almost every industry sector. Women responding to our survey span every aspect of the business world from individual contributor to business owner. Our survey sought professional women working in every role regardless of their profession: customer facing, teaching, management, human relations, finance, operations, technical, healthcare, and production.

Outside of work, women in our survey are equally busy and engaged as parents, in relationships with others, or on their own. Two-thirds of the women told us they have children.

Janice has two and Janet has no children. Not having children can be by choice or by chance; in Janet's case it is a bit of both, Mother Nature did not allow her to have children and she did not adopt.

Most are in some sort of committed relationship – married, in partnership, or comparable, along with us. A quarter of the survey respondents live independently, as singles or separated – widowed, divorced, split, or never married.

For more detail about the women responding to our survey browse through *Appendix 1: Strength of the Voices.*

Describing life beyond the thick-of-it

As professionals, we know how to describe our work-world experience by industry segment, functional area of responsibility, or leadership role. That all-important, time-consuming feature of our lives called work is easy to define. But how do we think about or describe ourselves beyond the thick-of-it?

Hungry to know more, we reached inside, interested to know what is going on behind the scenes – the connections, revelations, impact, and even the fears. We asked all of the women in our survey, "How do you refer to life <u>after</u> being in the thick-of-it?"

Across all three work-world relationships the women responding to our survey provided a description.

Women working on my-own-terms and out-of-the-paid-work-world describe where they are. They define the possibilities that exist within their current personal and professional life. There is a strong sense of identity, knowing who they are, and what they can do.

In contrast, women in the thick-of-it put a name on possibilities that lie ahead, looking ahead to the future. Those possibilities may lay at their feet, where they are, or be waiting for them at some time to come, when they choose to embrace them.

All the women we connected with share common characteristics. They are high-achieving, authentic, willing to commit themselves, and continuously endeavor for work-life balance. Their specific relationship to the work-world gives each a distinctly different character.

The work-world is a key reference point used by all the women in our survey. The biggest surprise is that women in every work relationship provide very similar descriptions, in near equal volume, although they may express it in slightly different ways.

In the responses to this open-ended question, we discovered two distinct threads in how women describe life after being in the work-world. One is an affirmation of "a new me" and the other is a comparison to the work-world.

The new me

"New me" is a revelation, a delightful surprise. A new identity emerges in how women describe the possibilities available to them. More than half of women in our survey describe it as a "new me".

Many refer to life after the thick-of-it as the next chapter, phase, stage, or beginning, even a new career. There is a sense of anticipation and affirmation where they can look ahead to what's next and acknowledge what's there.

There is also a strong sense of self and personal power: my time, my life, my choices. A step beyond life entangled with external requirements into life guided more from within.

Woven throughout this "new me" is a sense of joy: living life to the fullest, living in the moment, and spending more time with people and things most cared about.

> *Janet's "new me".*
> I completely identify with the majority of women who describe this as the "new me" – living fully, me time, the next chapter, or a new career. The "new me" was me as I worked for seventeen years on my-own-terms.
>
> Now that I am out-of-the-paid-work-world, it is a "renewed me". I embrace life with optimism and to the fullest. It doesn't mean that I don't go through periods of self-doubt, questioning, and confusion, but I welcome this new me.

In some ways, the "new me" described by women in the survey isn't all that different from a comparison. To have a new me, there must be an "old me" somewhere. In the "new me" is a freshness – new, different, not previously known. In the "old me" is the knowledge, experience, and

17

expertise to build upon. As you read ahead, listen to their collective voice, in their own words.

In this chapter, each ∞ infinity loop indention-with-distinction represents the words of multiple women. Each sentence is a different woman's voice as if you were standing in a small group discussion, each uniquely communicating their point of view.

Next. Within the "new me" group, half describe it as: "Next phase. Next chapter. Next act. Next stage. Next adventure."

Women in the thick-of-it express "Next" with movement.

∞ Change in pace. Lifestyle change (heard repeatedly). Moving on. New options. Part two. Shifting focus. Phase four. Simplifying life. A new season. Flexibility time (repeated like an echo within the hills).

Women working on my-own-terms have a sense of awakening.

∞ New reality. Getting on with life. Second half. Gap years. Changing focus. Shifting priorities. Encore years. (Hmmm, we wonder if this woman read May Sarton's book, *A Journal of the Eightieth Year.*)

Women out-of-the-paid-work-world have stepped into a new arena.

∞ Mid-life-gap-years. Moving on. My "after" life. New beginnings. Taking a risk to do something different.

Next Career. A quarter of the women expressing a "new me" describe it as: "Second career. My next career." In addition to these repeated descriptions, women in each work-related category described something else.

In the thick-of-it, women look at the future possibilities.

∞ New career portfolio. Next challenge. Painting on the beach. Interesting projects. Starting my 'lifestyle' business. Activity alteration. Time to garden and travel. Self-created, self-defined endeavors. Activism. Choosing to work for pay or not. Encore career. (Hmmm, several women may have read Marci Alboher's book, *The Encore Career Handbook*.)

Working on my-own-terms, women describe where they are.

∞ My third career. Flexibly working. Staying engaged. Pre-tirement. Committed to a broader set of activities. Redirecting my interests and abilities. Having the freedom of choice to work. Selectively working on what suits me. Move from the traditional work-world.

Women out-of-the-paid-work-world define themselves by what they are doing.

∞ Ski bum. More time for gardening. I work but don't get paid for it. I'm an author. Late in life stay at home mom. Managing my investments. Opportunity to travel. Community volunteer. Not working but still engaged. Strangely busy and always occupied. Freedom to combine personal pleasure and non-profit work.

Me time. A fifth of the "new me" women see life after the thick-of-it as "me time", a time to indulge themselves. "My time" echoes loudly. "Personal time. My time, all the time. Official ME time. Time for me."

In the thick-of-it, women see it as time for self-care.

∞ Slow down time. Answering to myself. Being able to do what I want. Living on my terms. More focus on health and leisure. Owning my own time. Unrestricted time to do what I want. Tuning in. Regroup. Caring for myself.

Working on my-own-terms, women set their own pace.

∞ Loving what I do, doing what I love. Preferred activities plan. Do as-and-when-I-like time. More freedom of choice to pursue my own and my husband's agenda. Managing my own time. Time to fulfill personal goals. Freedom to do what I want, with who I want, for what I care about. Define my day.

Women out-of-the-paid-work-world control their world.

∞ Doing what I want to do. Having time to myself. Nobody makes me go or do something I don't want to. Relaxing. Whatever the hell I want. Time for myself. What I want, when I want. Freedom to choose, without constraints.

Life renewed. The balance of women envisioning a "new me" split the description as "life" or "renewed".

"Life" – así es la vida – que sera, sera.

∞ My life. A finer life. Living. Ideal lifestyle. More relaxed lifestyle. My incredibly blessed life.

"Renewed" - Adapt, change, or refresh.

∞ Reinvention. Repurposing. Re-wiring. Redirection. Rediscovery. Redefined. Reinvigorated. (Read back through this list without the "re".) Young old. Self-actualization (we wondered if this meant some sort of guru status?).

Comparative

The comparative description makes a direct connection to the work-world being left behind. In our surveys, we asked for the sequel, "How do you refer to life <u>after</u> being in the work-world?"

In the entertainment industry, many sequels to movies are even better than the originals. Sequels like *Godfather Part II, The Empire Strikes Back,* and *Toy Story 3* remain on the top of great movie lists. When sequels are better than the original, it's because the director successfully builds on the story and the characters. We think that each of us are the producer and director of our own life's movie.

If you have ever been addicted to a book or TV series, it's because the storyline builds on the original in a meaningful way. It's a bit like the progression of our own lives: who you are today is the sequel to your past. Learning, knowledge, and experience builds upon itself so that the next chapter in our personal and professional story is different and (hopefully) better than the one before.

Yes, there are also bad sequels … and lots of them. But you don't have to see or indulge in them. It's your personal choice. Skip the bad sequel. You are the producer and director of your own movie.

One third of the responses directly address their sequel as a comparative to the intensity of working full-time.

Half describe the "NOT".

∞ No longer working. Not working for money. Post corporate life. Leaving the workforce. Stop working full-time. Quit. Done. Stepping away from day-to-day work. Leaving the corporate world. Post-career. Not punching the clock. Not having to work.

The other half of the responses describe the contrast.

∞ *Versus*. No schedule. Not having appointments every day. Out of jail. Released. Work without stress. Liberated. Done with the 50- to 70-hour work-week. Un-scheduled. Easing up. Not having to rush about. Doing something different. Not mandatory. The back nine (off the course, heading to the club house).

∞ *Transition*. Work with flexibility. Career change. Career break. Life transition. Scaling back. Focusing on other priorities. Break from 'the grind'. Released. Transition to the next interesting phase in my life.

∞ *Reward*. Celebrating my work life. Graduating. Permanent vacation. Sabbatical. Warriors' rest. Getting my just rewards. Extended vacation. A promotion. Sigh of relief.

The comparative definition makes sense. Our professional lives are fulfilling, rewarding, and demanding. As we consider what follows, the pre-and-post comparison is important: before and after, stress and less stress, demands yet flexibility. There is also a comparison in time: today and tomorrow, yesterday and today, or even three dimensions: yesterday-today-tomorrow.

The outliers

We don't want to leave any woman's perspective behind, so here's what the remaining respondents had to say.

Free. "Free" expresses the impact of changing our relationship with the work-world. "Free" expresses the influence it has on our life, our choices, and our sense of self.

There is a feeling of release.

> ∞ Freedom. Free time. Freedom of choice. Time of freedom. Freedom62. Freedom85. (We don't know what the numbers refer to but it might be the age of discovery.)

There is freedom wrapped in joy and consciously living in the present.

> ∞ Happiness. The good life. Enjoyment. Living and enjoying life in the moment. The best time of my life. My incredibly blessed life. Free to do whatever my heart's content. Time of fulfillment.

Many see it as freedom to play.

∞ Fun. On recess … on the playground. Playtime. Every day is Saturday.

Others see the expansion.

∞ Looking for my next adventure. A time for more exploration. Inspirement. Free to explore and define my days.

Ha-ha! We think that maybe freedom is a new TGIF experience. Let's unpack the acronym in a new way for our age of freedom. Thank goodness I'm free. Thank goodness it's fun. There I go fearlessly. The grand impetus freedom. This gal is fantastic. To gather in friendship. This gets incredibly fabulous. Toes go in first.

Retired. Like the overwhelming majority of the women in our survey, we don't like the word "retired" and choose to only use it sparingly. It is a convenient label, but it has far too much baggage in our opinion. Besides, leaving the paid work world completely is only an option, not inevitable.

There is no such thing as retirement.

∞ I don't refer to it. I don't use the word. I never refer to it. Wishful thinking. Not going to happen.

A few women out-of-the-paid-work-world were indignant or nearly belligerent about it.

∞ I always use the word 'retired'. I can't think of any other way to refer to it. There is no better word. I proudly use the word retired. What's wrong with the word? I like the Spanish word for retirement – jubilación!

24

UGH. A loud "UGH" was voiced from a small number of those in the thick-of-it and working on my-own-terms. An exclamation of disgust or horror. Their worst fears. "Boring. Boredom. Burnout. End of life. Inactivity. Non-reality. Old age. Closing down."

Yes, The Age of Freedom

The age of freedom emerges as the overarching theme that describes how women in each work-world category define the possibilities available to them.

Janice saw it immediately. Freedom instantly jumped off the page for her. It didn't matter that only a few of the women actually use the word "free" or "freedom". It best captures the essence of how professional women look at where we are and the possibilities that lay before us.

- The freedom of the comparative: "I can be this **or** that; I can even be this **and** that."
- The freedom of the new me: "I can refine, redefine, and invent myself – if I choose."
- The freedom to be free: "To be present, to play, to expand."

The *Age of Freedom* does not exclude or leave behind the women who are proud to be "retired" or shout "UGH" through the hallway. They are free to express themselves and be who they are. That is the beauty of it.

The *Age of Freedom* is not about "age"– the length of time a person has lived. It's about "age" as stage or epoch – a period of time marked by notable events and particular characteristics.

We think we may have done it! We have figured out how women describe the possibilities available to them. The age of freedom **IS** how we describe ourselves.

Women in the age of freedom are a beautiful and complex combination of … who we are, what we do, where we are going, and why we do what we do.

---

*It takes courage to grow up
and become who you really are.*
E.E. Cummings – American poet, painter, playwriter

Chapter 3

Let Your Reach Exceed Your Grasp

Working on my-own-terms means having flexibility to meet the demands of daily life in a new way.

If you are not in the thick-of-it, where are you? Are you in the "thin" of it? Or is there no longer an "it"? It's not "thin" and there definitely is an "it". Yes, still working. Continuing to be engaged and stimulated. Women working on-my-own-terms are most likely working in the same field, and some women venture into something new and entirely different. There are goals and objectives with important things to achieve.

Working on my-own-terms changes the terms and conditions of the work contract, bonding work and life in a new way. It is continuing to do something you love, or perhaps finding a new love. Both of us love working on my-own-terms. Janice has done it for eight years and counting. Janet enjoyed the seventeen years she worked on my-own-terms but recently stepped out-of-the-paid-work-world.

No matter where you are in your relationship with the work-world, let your reach exceed your grasp. Allow yourself to reach beyond the obvious and into your wants, wishes, and dreams. There are goals to be made. Objectives to be accomplished. Things to achieve. Do it on your-own-terms. Let your age of freedom shine.

Let it be YOUR time to do what YOU want.

- ∞ I gave myself permission to do what I want.
- ∞ Do as and when I like time.

Find work that suits you.

- ∞ Love what I do and doing what I love.
- ∞ I enjoy being involved in my professional field.
- ∞ I want to contribute where I can.
- ∞ I still love what I am doing.

Take a break, a breather, respite, or wind down.

- ∞ I stepped out of the work-world calling it my 'mid-life-gap-year'.
- ∞ I intentionally gave myself time to rest, reboot, and experience new things until I found a new path. Time down.

Our survey is a snapshot in time. At the time of our survey, a quarter of the women were actively working on my-own-terms. They are working, but maybe not full-time. Some are taking a sabbatical. They could be focused on developmental or experiential learning. They may have stepped in and out of the thick-of-it, one or more times. They are creating their own work-life balance.

Relationship to Work-World

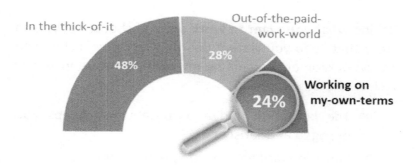

The lines blur. In a graphic image like the one above, it looks so definitive; so absolute. But it's not. Had we asked the questions a bit differently in the survey, we suspect that a good share of the women in the thick-of-it would consider themselves to be working full-time on my-own-terms. Many women step in and out of these work relationships as needed.

We will uphold the seemingly straightforward work-world classifications of the survey. But please read between the lines. If you are in the thick-of-it or out-of-the-paid-work-world, there are insights that will apply to where you are or where you are going in your own personal age of freedom.

Embrace the opportunity

One woman summed up working on my-own-terms perfectly: "I define it as working on **what** I want, **when** I want, and **with whom** I want." Let's explore this more deeply.

Decide <u>what</u> you want to work on. You choose to work in areas that keep you vibrant, learning, growing, active and involved. Women working on my-own-terms are in widely varied fields.

- ∞ The key is to find a purpose which keeps you engaged and satisfied.
- ∞ I look forward each day to doing what I do.
- ∞ I enjoy having the challenge to my thinking, personal growth, and the sense of purpose that my work provides.
- ∞ I am still learning.

Redefine yourself, changing professional direction as needed.

- ∞ I consider myself 'retired' from my first twenty-year career.
- ∞ I made enough money and no longer liked the day-to-day.
- ∞ I am pursuing a second different career.

Redefine <u>when</u> to work. No longer the predictable 8-10-12-hour day as previously defined or demanded by a company, organization, or even yourself. You can sleep in. You can work late. You can work that 8-10-12-hour day if you choose. The brilliant thing is that you can be involved at a higher level, not as burdened by as many transactional requirements.

- ∞ I flex around my other interests or my family's schedule.
- ∞ I am still professionally active, perhaps on a higher level since I am not committed to a 40-hour work week.

Dial it up or dial it down. It's nice to have the controls at your fingertips to turn the brightness up or down depending on what the work is and what else is going on in your life at the time. It's your choice.

- ∞ I am self-employed and can work in short (or long) spurts without feeling like work controls my life.
- ∞ I am able to work a minimal (or maximum) amount.
- ∞ I spent 8 months deciding to go back to work per diem. Per diem employees work on an as-needed basis, have a flexible schedule, and typically do not receive benefits.

There is more flexibility to select <u>who</u> to work with. Choose to work with organizations and people of similar ethics and business values, and as one woman said, "connect with wonderful people."

- ∞ I relish the opportunity to spend time with a more diverse and more creative set of individuals after leaving the corporate scene.
- ∞ I love my work of teaching and meeting new people as students.

∞ I may receive an offer to design a show that intrigues me and has the right group of people.

It is a pleasure to work with people and organizations that you both like and respect. We like people for any number of reasons: their sincerity, their openness, their curiosity and positivity, among other things. We respect people for their insight, intelligence, abilities, and experience. It's possible to have one without the other, but the most powerful combination is when we both like and respect someone. It's the same with organizations; we prefer to work for an organization where we like and respect the work it's doing.

Redefine where and how to work. COVID-19 was a game changer, redefining where and how we work. The mandate to work in the office, at home, at a client's office, on the road, or at a coffee shop is under your control more than ever. As one woman says, "I love the flexibility." You can work face-to-face or via video, conference call, text, or email.

You can even unplug, if you choose. On my-own-terms is considered a sabbatical for some, but not in the traditional definition of extended leave from a full-time career. It can also be defined as an active pursuit of purpose, according to remoteyear.com. What do YOU want to do?

∞ I am an RN (registered nurse) with burnout; I don't know if I want to go back into nursing or healthcare.

∞ I am comfortable as a stay-at-home mom at age forty-six.

∞ I may go back to school for a change in career.

∞ I have it made; I am able to work some, do all my fun creative activities, and spend time with family and friends.

∞ I can explore opportunities and fix up my house.

Working on my-own-terms means different things to different women. Well, it's YOUR terms, not anyone else's. You get to define and negotiate the terms of this 'contract', and your terms will be unique to you, different from others.

What does it mean to work on my-own-terms?

There are two fundamental components to working on my-own-terms: work and your terms. Miriam Webster says that work is a mental or physical activity as a means of earning income; employment. Thanks Miriam, you're correct. There really are three interconnected components: work, your terms, and getting paid. We will address getting paid in greater depth within the next section: Motivation.

As one woman told us, "Retirement is an outdated social construct that needs to be reworked for the current environment; a big part of this is to remove the imperative to retire." Thus, we discover working on my-own-terms!

The type of work is up to you. It may be a continuation of what you are doing in the thick-of-it or it may be something entirely new. If it's a continuation, it's because you love what you do. Or maybe you don't exactly love what you do, but you like it, and your expertise, skill, experience, and know-how are highly regarded and even sought after. Or maybe it's time for a change: you're burned out, tired, bored, or just ready for a new adventure.

The terms of your 'contract' can be written or implied. The agreement is between you and yourself.

The seven W-H questions are essential elements of your 'contract'.

- Who
- What
- Where
- When
- Why
- How
- How much

How much detail or importance you place on each question is at your discretion. Perhaps some aren't even worthy of consideration, as far as you're concerned. The COVID-19 pandemic forced each of us to review and revise our "contract" in some way.

> *Janet's seven W-H questions:*
> When I first broke out of the thick-of-it, the terms of my 'contract' with myself were pretty simple. The who-what-where were start-up companies in Silicon Valley that needed sales assistance. When-why-how-and-how-much were straight forward with a pretty standard 40- to 60-hour work-week doing what I love and letting the client set the fee structure.
>
> It evolved quickly as I learned more about myself, my clientele, and the world of working on my-own-terms.

From myself I learned that I preferred to work collaboratively, rather than alone. I prefer to work at the client's office rather than at home, if possible, as I could learn faster about the client's business and their needs. I prefer to work in concert with others; for me, the collective intelligence of a small group or a team far exceed the creativity and results of me alone. With every client I asked to be teamed with one or more key people. This is also how I moved from being a 'lone' consultant to co-founding a thriving consulting team.

From my clientele I learned how to structure my capabilities into 'products' with tangible outcome and results that clients were willing to pay for. It's hard to think of yourself as a 'product' but this was important in constructing a strong viable consulting practice. I also learned that I could do many things but had to 'position' my services around a strong singular area of expertise. I didn't leave my broader skill-set behind; it would emerge as the mutual trust and relationship with the client grew.

In this new world of working on my-own-terms, I learned how to value myself. It was a breakthrough of sorts. When I started out, I asked the client to set the fee; it was difficult for me to price my services. Then an "AH-HA" hit me: price my services based on the value of the results. Yes, a value-based fee structure that could be set based on the expected results or a project-based fee structure.

The next "AH-HA" was to price my services based on market value. Understanding what the typical salary-benefit package of a VP Sales in the client's industry, I priced my services accordingly. This fee structure is never disputed or argued. It also gave me the flexibility to charge by the hour or the 'professional day', based on the work to be accomplished.

The beauty of working on my-own-terms was that I could adjust every aspect of the 'contract' to suit my lifestyle, work-style, and the businesses I served.

This agreement can be changed at any time. You can add, change, delete, expand, and modify it to suit yourself. Write it down if that helps you clarify your thinking and agreement with yourself, but you don't have to.

One aspect of working on my-own-terms is getting paid for the work you do. The level of income is determined by the work you choose and the hours or effort you apply. You can adjust the income level based on your needs and wants. Necessity or opportunity can dictate the earnings when you are working on my-own-terms.

Income associated with the work you do is where the line blurs between being out-of-the-paid-work-world and working on my-own-terms. Many women out-of-the-paid-work-world consider themselves to be working, it's just that no income is involved. They are volunteers, interns, working pro bono, donating their time, or doing charity work.

How to begin working on my-own-terms

Everyone has a story. There are many different mechanisms that can start you working on my-own-terms. There are as many different catalysts as there are people, just ask for a story. How a woman comes to working on my-own-terms can be planned, unplanned or even a surprise. How we come to work on my-own-terms is intertwined with our motivation.

Why not! Indeed, why not work on my-own-terms, instead of someone else's. You can do it. Perhaps someone approaches you with the idea, and you think "Why not?" Or perhaps it's a clear choice, "Cutting back – first to half, now one-third time." The choice doesn't necessarily need to be accompanied with extensive preparation or planning. It could just feel right, so you go for it!

Ann B told us, "I was retired involuntarily about eight-years ago; I started substitute teaching and now work full-time; I am ready to sub again and then slide out of the work-world when my husband retires."

> *Donna W's story:*
> I was working full-time and thinking about breaking out on my own to do consulting work. I didn't have enough nerve to make the leap but it was there in the back of my head rattling around for a couple of years. I even changed my approach to my full-time job, tackling it with a consultant's mindset.
>
> Taking on a 'consulting mindset' gave me clarity around projects that I was working on. I set more specific goals and refined program deliverables. One

project no longer blurred and morphed into the next, seemingly without end. It successfully went on like this for several years.

Then POW, one day I got laid off. I was devastated. I didn't want to be unemployed. I immediately started interviewing for jobs. In one interview I was asked if I would take the job as a consulting assignment – how discouraging. I wanted a job. I went to bed that night feeling depressed and dejected.

Then POW, I woke up realizing that I was a consultant and this was my first client.

Interesting, I can do that. Seeing others successfully working on my-own-terms can provide the spark. It might be a role model, pace-setter, or someone doing something that you would like to. Role models have an important effect on our lives, shaping our behavior, decisions, and relationships.

Kimmy B's story:
It didn't take me long to start working on my own. I have a very entrepreneurial spirit. I don't like being told what to do and I like using my creativity. After cosmetology school I worked in a salon for another woman who mentored me. She really taught me a lot and showed me that it was possible.

I knew right from the start that I wanted to work on my-own-terms. It's been fifteen years now. I set my own schedule and can follow my interests. I opened a yoga studio while maintaining my salon business. I have been able to take a month off to hike the John Muir Trail. My line of organic skin care products is selling well. My boyfriend and I have a thriving organic farm. With COVID, I have moved into my own space creating a totally organic spa and salon. And I know there is more to come, I am only thirty-eight years old.

It just happened. Perhaps working on my-own-terms comes as a bit of a surprise. "I was offered a fun and not overly demanding non-executive trustee role." It can occur seemingly by chance. But perhaps it is more organic, a natural outcome. "I have relevant, unique, and in-demand skills."

Janet's story:
Did I choose to work on my-own-terms or did it choose me? I don't really know.

It started when I chose to leave my first start-up company, after seven exhilarating and all-consuming years. I loved that company; I helped to shape, form, and build it. I loved the people; they were my family, best friends, and biggest adversaries. I loved the challenge, the disappointment, the learning, and so much more. But it was time to move on.

I left my first start-up company because I didn't think I had enough new good ideas to continue building, forming, and growing it. So, as the founding VP Sales that took the company from ideas in a PowerPoint deck to a successful IPO (initial

39

public offering), I architected a graceful departure. I didn't quit, I 'fired' myself.

I didn't really think much about what was next. I knew I needed some down-time, but I was still full of piss and vinegar. I love working.

Almost immediately my network kicked into action. I was called by a friend and colleague who was working at another start-up company that was struggling to connect their products with customers. No, I was not ready to jump back in full-time. I needed to recharge my batteries. But, yes. YES, I would help. And so, seventeen years of successfully working on my-own-terms began.

Opportunity knocks. The most common thread is that an enticing work opportunity presents itself. It is fortuitous. "People request my services." "I frequently get calls from former colleagues to work on projects lasting from three months to two years." "The occasional project shows up that I am interested in helping with."

For some women, an associate pulls them into partnership on a business venture. "I have part ownership and interest in the company; I like the flexibility that I have." "My husband started a new company, so I work with him on a part-time basis." This is the power of Sheryl Sandberg's book *Lean In*. Our colleagues, co-workers, friends, and family reveal opportunities and encourage us in our endeavors.

Anonymous story:
I left my full-time job three years ago. I was asked immediately by two previous work associates to work on projects at two different companies. Three years later, I'm still working with one of those companies. My husband and I moved. So, I am now easing out of the work-world. I don't know if I want to leave the work-world entirely or continue working some hours per week.

Forced to look for other options. Some professions have mandatory retirement ages like pilots, law enforcement officers, national park rangers, air traffic controllers, and firefighters. Still wanting more, these women look for other options. "I haven't got time to not work; there's too much to do." "I have too much energy and too many interests."

Some professions provide retirement options after a number of years of service, like government workers, teachers, politicians, and career military. Missing the advantages of work, these women look for other work options.

∞ I like being out of the house, meeting people and need the money to supplement my pension.

∞ It helps me to structure my time and provides me with an answer to the question: 'What do you do?'

∞ Working part-time keeps me occupied and in contact with people.

The pandemic affected many businesses, demanding a reduction in staff, forcing many employees to look for other options.

It's my choice, not by chance. Make the choice and make it happen! As one woman says, "Plan early ... work as long as you can ... keep yourself young and active." And another, "Work gives me a routine, as much as I don't want to be getting up early every morning, I might get a bit lazy otherwise."

Janice's story:
Hand on heart, I knew after corporate life, I would make the decision to work on my-own-terms. I just didn't know how I would get there.

My professional career in the tech world had many adventures; three start-ups, two that went bust and the third that launched my career. It was fortuitous that the first two start-ups disappeared, because during that time I had my first son. The time off gave me a chance to sit back, take a year off, and decide my next move.

I settled comfortably into my third job and had good success during the first nine years. I was given the opportunity to move to Asia, so we packed up the family, now with two sons, and off we went.

Another decisive moment was when that company was acquired. After helping integrate the business into the new venture, I left that company to start my fourth career, still based in Asia.

My plan was to advance my career to an executive level. Once I achieved that, I told myself I would "retire". It took me four years to achieve that goal.

Then, it was time to go home, back to North America.

One year before my decision to move back, I reconnected with Janet in Asia. The burning question she had for me was: "What are you going to do when you get home? Call me."

That was the pivotal and serendipitous moment. The company I worked for wanted me to stay on in a new role back in Silicon Valley. I said, "No." Instead, I started my practice, reconnected with like-minded professionals, like Janet, and never looked back.

I was pretty scared to be out on my own. Would my clients and partners see the value I could bring? I was afraid of leaving the sanctuary of the corporate world, but I knew that I could grow and learn — learn the new ways of business and more importantly learn about myself.

Working on my-own-terms gives me choices. It gives me the flexibility to say no. It gives me back my time and lets me reinvent myself in ways I never thought possible.

Being self-employed is not for everyone

Working on my-own-terms doesn't necessarily mean being self-employed but it is an option for many.

Many women working on my-own-terms are employed in a paid work agreement with an employer. These women agree to provide certain services in return for being paid. The agreement can be full-time, part-time, as-needed, or on a project/piece-work basis. Benefits may or may not be part of the work agreement. As a professional, we implicitly understand this. Our work experience has equipped us to understand how to effectively manage the employer-employee work environment.

Being self-employed is different. Being self-employed doesn't work for everyone. You work solely for yourself. It's the toughest boss you will ever have! It's possible that your boss (YOU) will micromanage, not give you enough direction, or give you too much direction. It could also be the best boss you have ever had! Your boss (YOU) will intimately understand your needs, will advocate for you, and will promote work-life balance.

> *Roberta P thrives in an environment with structure.* After eleven years with the same company, they were going through some organizational changes and I was one of them. They gave me a very generous exit package with bonus and benefits enough to cover six-months. I started interviewing but wanted the right job and was in no real hurry.
>
> My first client was one that I worked with before, at the company I just left. It just sort of happened. The contract was lucrative, the work was something I knew well, and I could involve other experts in the contract work. It was almost too easy.

It's amazing what I began to learn. I learned what an optimal work environment is for me. I found that I missed working in an office setting. Working from home I am significantly more productive without all the distractions. But it is lonely and there is no one to bounce ideas off of; no chatter about new business trends at the coffee machine or over lunch, and there are distractions that are not work related.

At work I was always praised and recognized for being self-motivated, determined, and self-directed. What a perfect combination for working on my-own-terms … or so it seemed.

Working for yourself is a blank sheet of paper. There are no restrictions. The possibilities are endless. How wonderful to be able to do whatever I wanted. But it is daunting. How to choose what direction? What if I made the wrong decision? I would 'what if' myself to a screeching halt. I quickly learned that my strength is as a situational leader: put me in a structured environment and I can quickly determine how to make the most of it, improve performance and optimize outcome.

I need a sandbox to play in. I am at my best when I understand the boundaries. I may need to keep the sand inside the sandbox but I can shoot for the stars and dig to China. I may even test the borders of the sandbox, but give me a sandbox to play in and I can build a sand castle that will shine.

Working for myself, being self-employed, was not for me. That first client contract went well but I

45

immediately went back to find my next sandbox, happy with pail and shovel in hand.

If you are self-employed, you are a sole proprietor, a freelancer, independent contractor, consultant, or coach. The job flexibility and autonomy are unmatched, but there are risks and income volatility.

Being self-employed is being the sole operator of your business. You manage income, expenses and benefits; and you pay taxes. You may work with or "hire" other independent contractors to work with you on projects. Being self-employed is not the same as being a business owner who hires employees.

When you are self-employed, you contract directly with customers and clients. Pause and think about what this means.

- You source, promote, and find work for yourself (marketing and business development).
- You prepare the work proposal, price the work, and close the deal (sales).
- Then the work begins, and you perform the job to be done (execute).
- When the work is finished you collect payment (billing and collections).
- You will ask for a referral, references, and repeat business (customer success management).

Dana Y loves work but hates business development. I wanted the freedom and flexibility of working for myself. I had been working independently for almost two years. I designed my business around my area of expertise because I love the work I do.

But I hate finding new clients. My work flow and income had tremendous peaks and valleys. When I have a client project, I am happy, work hard, delight my client, but don't do any business development.

When the project ends, I hear crickets. There is a long dry spell with no work while I go out looking for new clients. Then the cycle starts over again. I hate business development. I love the work. I hate selling and marketing myself.

I had to face the facts; it was better for me to work for someone else. I could do what I love, without all that extra stress and worry.

Another woman in our survey agrees with Dana Y: "I am only fifty-eight years old and enjoy what I do but don't like to market myself. If I can get work some other way, I am happy to do it."

Susan H loves work but hates billing and collections. Landscape design is my passion. I love the beauty of nature and creating special spaces for people. I don't care if it is a small intimate area or large and expansive; tapping into the needs of the client is the same process.

As a longtime Star Trek fan, I enjoy doing the Vulcan mind-meld with a client, really getting into their head. Understanding what they want to accomplish, how they will use it, the aesthetics, sight lines, sounds, and smells. I love the process of discovery, design, and delivering a genuinely pleasing setting.

Forgive me, but I hate billing and collections; I really suck at that. After leaving a lot of money on the table, I finally got smart enough to hire someone to do it for me. Yes, it adds to the cost of a project but after a while I figured out how to package it into the overall price. On to the next design job, problem solved.

Working on my-own-terms and being self-employed, is not for everyone. But it does succeed for many. Find your own unique path, listen to yourself, learn what works best for you. Be honest with yourself. Have a little heart and a sense of humor. Know that working on my-own-terms has the choice of working for yourself or working for others.

The motivation

Even with the vast wealth of research, literature, science, and theories on motivation, there are fundamentally two things that motivate us: survival or fulfillment. It's the yin and yang of what stimulates us, the negative and positive forces. On one end the driving factors are founded in fear and worry, on the other is self-realization, happiness, and contentment.

What motivates women to work on my-own-terms spans this range. Negative forces are the fear and worry of dissatisfaction, rejection, boredom, and not being able to

48

pay the bills. Positive forces are confidence and endeavors for meaningful work, stimulation, a stable future, and giving back.

These contrary energies push and pull at us. It is the complementary dualism of yin and yang. We can simultaneously worry about paying the bills and strive for a stable future. We want to minimize unpredictability and strengthen or secure certainty.

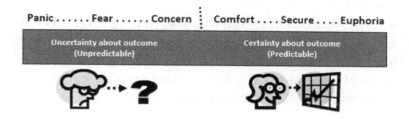

When a professional woman decides to move out of the thick-of-it to work on my-own-terms we think it's important to examine and understand what the motivation is.

Income is an important motivator

Compensation-systems are based on the principle of extrinsic reward. Pay grades, tenure, pay-for-performance, bonus structure, and commissions are well-defined examples. Whether you are paid by the hour, by the job, or based on results, money is an expected outcome.

- ∞ It's nice having money coming in.
- ∞ I like having some extra income.
- ∞ Financial reasons.

∞ It's simple, I need the money.

The nice thing about working is that income is associated with it. The income can be extra money to go toward immediate expenses or to tuck away for a specific purpose.

As professionals, the women in our survey have a degree of financial stability yet income remains a key motivation in their decision making.

The first motivational theories appeared in the early 1940's with the work of Abraham Maslow. Maslow's work is best known for establishing the hierarchy-of-needs. He classified human needs into a five-tier pyramid ranging from essential physical imperatives like food, water, and shelter moving upwards toward self-actualization.

The order of Maslow's hierarchy-of-needs begins at the base with physical essentials, safety, love and belonging, esteem, and self-actualization. When the needs of that tier are satisfactorily met, an individual can move to the next

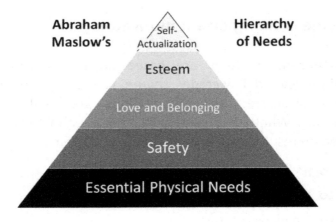

level. Originally Maslow believed that a lower level must be completely satisfied before moving on to a higher level. But today psychologists view these levels as overlapping and often operating in parallel.

Maslow's pyramid explains the need for money in a simple and straightforward manner. Income can be imperative to meet basic physical needs of food, water, and shelter. Income may be necessary to make ends meet and get the bills paid to satisfy essential needs. Or when income is used for pleasures beyond essential necessities, the motivation is to fulfill needs in the upper half of the pyramid.

Spending for survival needs is a critical obligation: housing, food, healthcare, and paying bills. Extra cash can provide an opportunity to splurge on things that are nice-to-have, desirable, or even impractical.

It is important to maintain cash flow.

∞ Healthcare.

∞ House payments.

∞ I don't want to tap into my long-term savings or investments in case I outlive my money.

Nina J's second career.
My husband and I both worked for the same company. He worked there long enough to qualify for a pension but I didn't. He was in a position with mandatory age retirement. The retirement benefits were good and we counted on them.

Then the company went through hard times and restructured their business. Restructuring their business meant restructuring our benefits, reducing them by two-thirds. Yikes! This was quite a blow.

My husband and I immediately reduced expenses and jumped back into the work-world. I work in travel and my husband in real estate. Our two new later-in-life careers give us flexibility along with the income we need.

We had not tucked enough away in savings to account for the reduction of company benefits. How could we have anticipated what occurred? It was unprecedented.

Extra cash can go into savings. It can be money for a "rainy day" expense or emergency fund. For people without company pensions or retirement benefits, it can pay for healthcare benefits, supplementing government programs and benefits, like U.S. Social Security or Canadian Social Insurance. Extra cash in savings may be for a specific purpose like a vacation, a house remodel, or a new car ... or maybe a boat, recreational vehicle, a motorcycle, or even an airplane.

Money to achieve long term goals or for a specific purpose.

- ∞ I haven't achieved my financial goals.
- ∞ I like making some money so it's not all from savings.
- ∞ I need the money for travel, and I like what I do.
- ∞ I still can get a few bucks and a few trips from my clients.

A desire to achieve financial independence to support the needs of a lifetime.

- ∞ Finalizing financial security.
- ∞ I'm still relatively young and want to make sure I'm financially stable for my later years.
- ∞ Need to make sure we have enough money to live a long time.
- ∞ I set out long ago to be part of the 'F.I.R.E' movement (financial independence, retire early). Spiritually I never felt suited for the world of white men in suits – that corporate setting where I spent the majority of my career.

The F.I.R.E. movement advocates maximizing income, savings, and investments while dramatically decreasing expenses with the goal of financial independence, so that paid-work becomes optional. The movement exploded out of Robin and Dominguez's 1992 best seller, *Your Money or Your Life*, and struck a chord with all ages, especially those in the twenty-five to forty-five age range. The movement seemed to peak in the early 2010s but served to introduce or restore financial management techniques to a broader range of people.

> *Janet sought financial independence.*
> Winding the clock over the twenty-five great years in the thick-of-it, I began working on my-own-terms. The income for daily living expenses and for the future were both important. I worked on my-own-terms for seventeen years. My husband and I were both in occupations with no pensions.

I was forty-seven years old when I started working on my-own-terms. It wasn't only about the money, I had energy and more to accomplish. At the time, I didn't need healthcare; I rode along on my husband's health benefit plan.

Planning for the future was always important to us. In our very early years together when money was tight, we kept a strict budget and put money into savings every month, even if it was only a small amount.

We tried to live on one salary, because we were concerned about the instability of the industry sectors that we were in. Our income stability grew rapidly, and those fundamental money management principles strengthened the confidence we had at the base of our financial pyramid.

Maintaining a strong profitable business on my-own-terms contributed significantly to the day-to-day household expenses as well as our long-term financial independence.

The nice thing about working is that there is a sense of predictability about income. A sort of working mathematical theorem — if A, then B. It's a story with a predictable plot, where we have a pretty good idea of what to expect. Hours, effort, or outcome equal income. If I work "this much", I can expect to receive "that much" income in return.

Women that are not comfortable with their financial position are more likely to remain in a structured work environment with more predictable income; they stay in the thick-of-it and in the employment of others.

Our survey targeted input from professional women at all stages of career and does not reflect the entire population of women. A relatively small percent of professional women in our survey are distressed about making ends meet. Conversely, in the general population of women, a report from the Canadian Imperial Bank of Commerce (CIBC), tells us that nearly two-thirds of Canadian women worry about their finances. Of those, younger women (18-34) are the most concerned and those financial concerns ease for women over fifty-five. Likewise, NBC News reports similar numbers for American women.

Women with more secure financial conditions are willing to work on my-own-terms and even make the leap into self-employment. With more financial security, women are willing to trade income predictability for time flexibility. There is also risk. Rewards rest on individual flexibility and the ability to adjust effort to fit, fulfill, or create the desired lifestyle.

> ∞ Even though I have good savings and a solid plan for when I leave the paid work-world, the idea of not having money coming in from work is a bit scary.

Income motivation is driven by urgency or confidence. In Maslow's hierarchy-of-needs, urgency drives fulfilment on the lower tiers of the pyramid. If there is confidence that the vital needs at the base of the pyramid are being met, then income drivers are focused on accomplishment in the upper tiers.

There is no reason to leave the work-world

Retirement is an archaic, outmoded concept.

> ∞ There is no need to leave the work-world. I don't ever want to fully leave it. In my mind, the word 'retire' is related to collecting social security. I still have a lot to offer and work has a lot to offer me.

Working on your-own-terms means working for yourself. The work may be in the employment of others, but the purpose is yours. The work may be structured by an organization, but the value and fulfillment is yours. Working on my-own-terms is more of a mindset: work for yourself, not for others.

How do you feel about where you are? Have you 'had it' with full-time employment – fed up, unsatisfied, frustrated, or bored? Do you have enough money to cover your basic needs? Do you have other pursuits that you would like to spend more time with?

> ∞ I decided to 'quit working' for others when I'd had enough, had enough (money), and had enough to do; if one cannot answer in the affirmative to all three of those 'had' questions, then stopping is not the answer.

Obligatory 'retirement' compels other possibilities. Some women working on my-own-terms are in vocations where retirement is compulsory or mandatory by the company, occupation, or age. Being required to 'retire' forces decisions, yet it opens up other possibilities.

∞ Finding myself 'forced' into retirement colors my perspective; but I enjoy choosing to work based on my own interests and needs.

Things outside of our control can mandate change.

∞ I am disabled and had to leave work full-time; I hope to increase my work hours as I enjoy the challenges and excitement of work.

∞ I would have worked longer if not for health issues; those same issues limit what I can do today.

The work-world is filled with energy, opportunity, and stimulation

What motivates us is driven by both internal and external factors. Sometimes it's hard to separate them as they push and pull together.

Internal motivation is intrinsic and comes from within. It can be for deep-rooted personal reasons that may be associated with our core values, our upbringing, religious beliefs, or subconscious factors. Internal motivators can be positive or negative, driving us for pleasure or out of fear.

External motivation comes from something outside of us. We do things because we are obliged or required to. External forces are norms, standards or regulatory systems in business, society, or government. It is something that has power over us. External forces can be something we respect and care about, or just the opposite.

The work-world is a powerful external motivator, and our relationship with it touches us deep-down inside.

The intellectual stimulus of the work-world is engaging.

- ∞ I like continuing to challenge myself.
- ∞ I like the intellectual challenge of my work coupled with a schedule that works for me.
- ∞ I am enjoying the work I do and staying connected to corporate mainstreams.
- ∞ I want to stay up with current trends/ideas. Not ready to lose relevance.
- ∞ Where else can I find the same level of inspiration? I am still learning.

The work-world provides an energy outlet.

- ∞ I have too much energy and too many interests.
- ∞ I worry about being bored.
- ∞ I'm surprised how easy it is to stay busy and interested without full-time work; I am rarely bored.
- ∞ I haven't got time; there is too much to do.

Working with other people is a joy.

- ∞ I stay curious, stay healthy, and connect with others.
- ∞ Working part-time keeps me occupied and in contact with people.
- ∞ I would be bored; I like the interaction, activity, and networking while continuing to work from home.

There are new and different fields of interest open to discovery.

- ∞ I am now involved in professional writing.

- ∞ I chose to become involved with our personal business affairs.
- ∞ My organic vegetable garden is growing into an organic farming business.

Working on my-own-terms wraps it all together. It's both personal and professional. It can satisfy the complementary duality of external and internal motivators, providing freedom and structure. Working on my-own-terms allays some fears and provides a sense of satisfaction as one woman details, "I enjoy having the challenge to my thinking, my personal growth, and the sense of purpose that my work provides."

If you love what you do, continue doing it!

A strong common thread woven throughout the comments of women working on my-own-terms is that their chosen field is something they love.

Continue to delight in your work.

- ∞ I enjoy being involved in my professional field.
- ∞ I enjoy what I do. I love my job.
- ∞ I enjoy the stimulus of meeting people and keeping my professional skills honed.
- ∞ I look forward each day to doing what I do.

Teaching is an especially rewarding career field.

- ∞ I missed teaching and went back to substitute teach when the opportunity arose.

∞ I enjoy the students and keeping up with educational trends.

∞ I love my work of teaching, seeing my long-time students, and meeting new ones.

Every professional field has its rewards.

∞ I enjoy being involved in the area of my professional background.

∞ I still love what I am doing and enjoy my work too much.

∞ I haven't found another interest I'd rather spend my time at.

∞ I am a managing partner of a venture fund, and still have a few portfolio companies yet to exit.

∞ Enjoying work, and feel I can contribute.

Some women look to accomplish more in their field of endeavor.

∞ Still have things left to do.

∞ I need to be involved in my business until the transition to the new owner is complete.

∞ I am still young and have more to accomplish.

∞ I enjoy contributing on a company board or two.

∞ There are goals I would still like to achieve.

"I love what I do" is echoed again and again by those working on my-own-terms.

> *Annmarie N is authoring her future.*
> I'm knee deep in my career and don't expect that to change anytime soon.

I love what I do. I love having an impact. Most importantly, I love that the work I do creates conditions for others to have an impact in their own professional or personal careers.

Moving forward, I think about the work I do today, and how I can do it on my-own-terms. I've also found that I've become pickier about where I invest my energy.

I am much less patient with the nonsense and much more possessive about my time. Ten years ago, I danced to the tune of what the corporate job dictated me to do. I didn't think twice of loading up my work calendar, double booking meetings, traveling five days a week – being tied to my job. Now, I'm not dancing to that tune anymore! I said no. It's just not going to happen that way anymore!

I'm physically in the thick-of-it, the thick of my career, but I'm also mentally rewiring. I refer to it as rewirement – because I'm not retiring, I'm rewiring.

Rewirement is taking everything about who you are, the contributions you want to make and where you want to put those contributions. I know I want to remain relevant in my career and my personal life, yet that relevance is being redefined.

My theme is around authoring my future as opposed to having society author it. I'm in the process of that, and I'm working with a couple of friends to think about how we take what we do, but do it in a venue that's <u>on our terms</u>.

Community involvement plays an important role for me today and in authoring my future. Looking at it broadly – I have "little c" and "BIG C" communities. My "little c" community revolves around my son. I sit on the Board of Trustees at his school, I volunteer in things he is interested and engaged in, because that's the community around him and I want those to be successful.

My "BIG C" community is where I spend most of my energy. It's focused on diversity and women in the workforce. It seems that the older I get, the more engaged I am around women's issues and helping them progress in their careers. Particularly women who are in the financial services market because it's a very male-centered profession and I'm also in private equity.

Authoring my future is all about doing it on my-own-terms, when I want, how I want and, where I want.

Make a contribution

Contributions made at work have significant impact. Having a sense of purpose and making a contribution operates in two directions, affecting us personally as well as those we serve.

Feeling that we are contributing promotes our sense of well-being. It provides a sense of purpose that is greater than ourselves and beyond our own self-interest. Having a sense of purpose and contribution in everything we do makes the time and effort seem worthwhile. This applies to any activity or action, no matter how big or small.

The value of the human connection: involving, linking, teaming, and collaborating.

- ∞ Helping people is a really high value of mine and I do that through my work.
- ∞ I love having more time to spend with people I care about, especially time with loved ones.
- ∞ I could probably find other ways to help people, but coaching is very 'me' and therefore one of the ways that I can give the most back to the world.

The importance of growth and learning: sharing knowledge and continuing to learn.

- ∞ With years of experience, professional women have so much talent to give back to the world, I don't see us just sitting around watching TV and playing golf all the time.
- ∞ Not sure that I will permanently leave the work world; I plan to remain relevant in both for-profit and non-profit organizations.

Contributing to the greater good, helping and assisting others to improve or achieve their goals: students, patients, clients, customers, or community.

- ∞ I want to contribute to the community.
- ∞ I consider myself retired from corporate life but continue to work in non-profit and public sector.
- ∞ I now serve on our town council.
- ∞ I am privileged to contribute to causes I believe in.

∞ I want to contribute where I can.

Women working on my-own-terms seek a healthy equilibrium. The healthy equilibrium is work-life balance, striving for symmetry with good measure on both sides of the scale. Working on my-own-terms allows for expansion beyond work to the world, where balance can extend into neighborhood, community, society, or beyond.

The "afterwork"

If there is an afterlife, life-after-life, maybe there is an "afterwork", work-after-work. We don't know if there is an afterlife, but it could be possible. We won't know until we get there, and maybe even then we won't know we are there.

We think that working on my-own-terms is the "afterwork" to being in the thick-of-it. Not the immediate afterwork of cocktails with friends or hitting the gym, but the longer horizon of work-after-working. The work can be in the employment of others or self-employed.

For some women, the afterwork could be staying in the thick-of-it, finding a new functional role or shifting into a new professional field.

The afterwork is nonlinear. It does not move only in one direction.

Time is linear where one second leads to one minute, one hour, one day, and one year. But life in general and work-life balance are not as regimented. Progress in not measured by time but by advancement and growth.

Time marches on. Without a time machine we cannot go back to an earlier era. You can't reverse time. There is no 'do over'. Life and work are different, they amply allow for reinvention. There is opportunity to restart and redo things in a different way – a second chance, another shot, a new opportunity, a retake, or a fresh start.

There are periods when work is a fox trot: two steps forward and one step back, still moving forward with a step back to add rhythm and bravura.

> *Janet's fox trot.*
> On multiple occasions in the thick-of-it I did a fox trot at work. I would take a job outside my area of expertise, or one with less leadership responsibility, or at lower pay because it would expand my business knowledge and move me forward.
>
> I reflect on when I climbed Mount St. Helens in Oregon after its volcanic eruption; that was also a fox trot. Volcanic ash is really a sea of rock marbles, with every step forward I slid backward a half step or more. I made it to the summit and stood on the edge of the crater in awe of the power of nature. The sea of volcanic marbles made the trip back down fast fun! It's amazing what we can accomplish in the fox trot of life and work.

Not knowing can reveal opportunity.

∞ I know there is more in me but I am not sure what the next opportunity will be; I will be more seriously looking in the next year.

Cycle in and out of the work-world at your bidding.

∞ I left a full-time private-sector job, cared for aging parents, and now have a part-time public-sector job: in a sense it is my encore career.

∞ I have translated my professional skill set into a great work-from-home role with wonderful flexibility and financial reward. I am less stressed and happier.

Companies benefit by tapping into experienced resources.

∞ Interesting that in my contracting work I have run into many women who have 'retired' one or more times and have been called back to work by their company, like I have.

∞ Companies aren't doing enough to backfill and train replacements; they need our expertise.

∞ One project I worked on had four of us 'returnees' – in HR, marketing, communications, and me in tech … interesting!

Fulfill your needs.

∞ I think there are two things key to leaving full-time employment: one, being psychologically prepared for the shift … guilt, boredom, friction in relationships that are hard to anticipate, and two, the 'bag lady' syndrome that causes many women to have financial anxiety, even if they shouldn't.

Eve J finds working on my-own-terms more lucrative. I am 82, am I too old for your survey? I keep three professional licenses active – law, real estate broker, and residential building contractor. Along with my boyfriend, I dabble in real estate, flip houses, and manage investment properties. The rental income supplements pensions nicely.

I worked full-time, in the thick-of-it as you would say, until I was 77-and-a-half. I wanted to pay off the house but I was falling asleep in business meetings. Feeling comfortable about money makes life easier. I already had my toe in life on the other side, doing some traveling and flipping houses.

The interesting surprise was that I made more money after leaving work. I also surprised myself and I just finished writing my first novel, *The Last President of the United States.*

My advice is to work as long as you can. Don't leave the work-world until you absolutely have to. Be debt-free if possible, pay off the credit card, the car loan, and the mortgage if you can; it takes the pressure off. And enjoy life! There is more fun to be had!

The "afterwork" doesn't happen in any set order; it's nonlinear. There is an interplay of competing and complementary backbones: paid-work versus unpaid work. You can move between the thick-of-it, on my-own-terms, and out-of-the-paid-work world, then back again.

Leslie C builds her own off ramp.
My professional career spans over twenty-years and I'm still at it. My executive career had me based in Indonesia, Japan, London and now in California. I love every minute of it.

I'm not ready to retire from my career. I still need to build more personal equity and a bigger nest egg before tapping into my savings. Besides, I thrive on my job and wouldn't change a thing about it. Even so, I started thinking about building my off-ramp.

I needed a plan. A plan that in four to five years would enable me to jump the chasm from my professional work life to something new, yet still offer a rewarding lifestyle for both me and my partner.

And now, although I am still hard at it and in the thick-of-it, I've become a goat rancher! Yes, a farmer! How in the heck did that happen, you ask?

I guess the pivotal moment was when my best friend suddenly died. It came out of nowhere. She and I were thick-as-thieves. We'd go on vacations together and Sunday dinners were built into our routine. My loss is still indescribable.

After losing my dear friend, I felt lost and bored. I knew I had to do something and fill in the empty times after work. So, I took a course on training sheltered dogs with the intent to get them ready for adoption. This got me thinking. How can I expand this joy and do something with animals? A casual visit to friends in

68

northern California propelled me and my partner into the idea of being ranchers!

Both me and my partner knew we were keen to add something in our lives. Ranching was nothing we ever dreamed of. We had no experience. Our high-tech careers didn't include a Ranching-101 course. But we were both excited and ready to take on the risk.

Our first step was meeting with our financial advisor. Her advice was: "You don't have to build your ranch the moment you retire. You have the financial means, start planning now. What are you waiting for? Just do it!"

Now we're in the thick-of-it, building out fifty acres! Never in my life did I imagine I would be a goat farmer. It brings me stability, professionally and personally. The mental stimulus I get from my current job is balanced with the physical effort of being a rancher.

It has also helped me be a better leader. I appreciate that work as we know it can't be the only thing important in our lives. It has made me understand that you can create a balance. You can be highly effective in your job, yet have something else in your life that motivates and brings new value to everything you do.

Being a goat farmer has also shown me the importance of being a lifelong learner. I entered a new world. I had to learn a whole new industry and vocabulary. I had to learn new skills required in managing goats, their health, and well-being. I had to immerse myself in the science of agriculture and the commercial aspects of running a ranch.

Planning my next career as a goat farmer wasn't only about building a financial plan. I had to consider the impact it would have on leaving my professional relationships behind. I had to think about the consequences of uprooting and moving to a new community.

I believe that one just can't finish a high-powered job and do nothing. I knew I had to have something to go to, a second work life. I realized early on, that unless I made it happen, it wasn't going to be waiting for me when I shut that corporate door behind.

My best friend's death was a catalyst that brought me where I am today. I recognize that it's never too early to build your own off-ramp. And, most importantly, if you're doing what you love, it's not work.

Take a fresh approach to the seven W-H questions. Consider the questions in a new light. Your answers to these questions are interconnected, changing, bending, and entwined with one another.

- **Effort**: Full-time, part-time, no-time (when and how much)?
- **Substance**: Type of work and the contribution (what and why)?
- **Engagement**: In the employment of others or self-employed (who and where)?
- **Composition**: Structure versus flexibility (how and where)?

Just like Leslie C, you can build your own off ramp and discover your "afterwork" on your own terms.

Chapter 4

Happiness, Wellness, and Healthcare

As years turn into decades, a big piece of our state of happiness is being healthy and having comfortable options for managing our health in the long-term.

We explore the topics below along with insights and stories from women who generously gave their time for interviews and answered our survey.

- Happiness and Cloud Nine
- What makes us happy?
- Lists, lists and more lists
- Pursuit of happiness
- Wellness and its impact to our health

- The many facets of healthcare
- An ideal healthcare system
- Top of mind concerns
- Our health check
- A full life

Happiness and Cloud Nine

Happiness is a state of well-being and contentment. It creates a sense of optimism, a positive attitude of "the glass is half full" where we think about the good things in a situation rather than the bad ones. It creates a positivity that can be infectious. Happiness is tied to our jobs, the lifestyle we choose, and our closest relationships. Happiness is also tied to how we take care of ourselves both in physical and mental health.

We seek happiness in various ways. It may be doing something selflessly for the good of others. Doing things that we are good at, like our careers which we take pride in. Doing things that are good for us, like taking care of our health and wellness. Doing things that we enjoy, like traveling, hobbies, volunteering, or socializing.

There are times when we may experience a perfect state of happiness, like being on Cloud Nine; a moment, event or situation that brings immense joy, giving us feelings of euphoria.

Janice's Cloud Nine moment.

During my time in Asia, I had the wonderful opportunity to travel to Bhutan, officially known as the Kingdom of Bhutan, a small country located in the Himalayas, bordered by Tibet, an autonomous region in China and India. This is a country which measures GNH – Gross National Happiness – over GDP. Their GNH Index is a holistic approach to measure the happiness and well-being of the Bhutanese population.

Bhutan's tagline, "Happiness is a place" perfectly encapsulates the philosophy of Gross National Happiness and simply assures that happiness can be found in simple things that can be found anywhere and in anything.

On my flight to Paro, Bhutan, I had the unexpected pleasure of meeting Mr. Lhaba Tshering, Chief Policy and Planning Division, Gross National Happiness Commission. To this day, I still have his business card because of its uniqueness and the position he holds for the country.

What an opportunity it was to sit next to this kind gentle man during the two-plus hour flight and learn how happiness forms the core values of Bhutan and its people. I remember asking him, "How does one measure happiness?" After all, I was working for a corporation that instilled in me – "If you can't measure it, you never really have done it!" So naturally I was curious to understand more. He shared that the Centre for Bhutan Studies just completed their 2010 survey (my visit was in 2011).

The questions in their survey explored ten aspects of how a Bhutanese citizen feels about their life.

1. The education system.
2. Their health.
3. The quality and access to health services.
4. Their psychological well-being.
5. How stressed they feel.
6. Time spent at work and at home.
7. Their trust in their neighbors and their government.
8. Their knowledge and awareness of environmental issues.
9. The level of confidence with cultural traditions and rituals.
10. How happy they feel.

I sat back in my seat and pondered how I would answer those ten questions, and what I would learn about myself and my own state of happiness.

The day before we left Bhutan, we attended the Thimphu Tshechu festival. Tshechus are grand events held at various towns throughout the year where entire communities come together to witness religious mask dances, receive blessings, and socialize.

We were told that the King of Bhutan, Jigme Khesar Namgyel Wangchuck, may be attending the festival that day. As I was sitting on the grassy hillside, waiting for the festival to start, a young girl of perhaps no more than 10 years old raced up to me. She wore a beautiful dress of silk and vibrant colors, but what I noticed most was the shine and sparkle in her eyes. She looked at me and said "Ma'am, are you happy today? I would like to make you even more happy! The King is coming, and I will take you to him. Come quickly and run with me so we can meet him together."

She took my hand and we clamored down the hill just as the King's humble procession was coming into view. She led me to the front of the area so we could be positioned to see him.

Then, suddenly, she jumped in front of the King with my arm in tow, and said: "Dear King Wangchuk, please meet my friend." And I did. He said, "Welcome to our country, we are honored to have you with us." WOW.

The best part was, when the young girl turned to me and asked: "Ma'am, are you happy now?" And indeed, I was. That was my Cloud Nine moment.

What makes us happy?

Thinking about what we most enjoy, what we look forward to, and what we would like to spend more time on: we asked women in our survey to choose their top three options from a list of ten. The options were the same for all the women in our survey: in the thick-of-it, working on my-own-terms, and out-of-the-paid-work-world:

1. Adventure related activities.
2. Creative or art activities (painting, writing, music, theater, etc.).
3. Community involvement.
4. Developing stronger relationships with family and friends.
5. Doing new things (and maybe stepping out of their comfort zone).
6. Improving health and physical fitness.
7. Personal development (learning and interests).
8. Professional-related activities.
9. Spending more time with hobby and interests.
10. Travel.

No matter where we are in our relationship to the work-world, all of us agree that travel is a top option. The global pandemic struck a blow to this top option. We will examine that more in the next chapter.

Developing stronger relationships with family and friends is important, ranking number-two for women in the thick-of-it and for those out-of-the-paid-work-world. Women on my-own-terms ranked family and friends as number-one, which means that personal relationships are a driving factor in how they shape their work-relationship.

Community involvement ranked in the top-four for women in the thick-of-it and out-of-the-paid work world. It slipped to number-five for women on my-own terms, telling us that while community involvement is still important, it does not take priority over other activities for these women.

Rank	In the thick-of-it	On my-own-terms	Out-of-the-paid-work-world
1	Travel	**Family & Friends**	Travel
2	Health & Fitness	Travel	**Family & Friends**
3	**Community Involvement**	Health & Fitness	Hobbies & Interests
4	**Family & Friends**	Personal Development	**Community Involvement**

While there are many factors that define our happiness, we can definitely correlate what we enjoy doing to our overall sense of contentment.

What degree of happiness would you place on the above options and why? For many of us, travel gives us happiness because it can enable us to learn and experience new things. Being with family and friends provides nurturing connections that are meaningful to our well-being. Community involvement gives us an opportunity to give back.

Take a moment and honestly rate your level of happiness right now on a scale of one to ten, with ten being the happiest. Where would you rate yourself? What factors or frame of reference are you using to define your own happiness? This can be dynamic based on the current situations you are facing, for example like the pandemic that is still prevalent in our societies.

If you are not approaching ten in your self-examination, maybe one place to start is to consider the questions that were asked in the Bhutan GNH survey in Janice's story above. Or simply re-examine the things you enjoy most and strive to do more of those things.

In a Harvard Business Review article titled "What Kind of Happiness do People Value Most?" the author, Cassie Mogilner Holmes, writes that Nobel prize winner Daniel Kahneman, makes a distinction between being happy _in_ your life versus being happy _about_ your life.

Sure, there are specific moments, or times that make us happy _in_ our lives. If we can, we will repeat those things that make us happy. This creates a comfortable cadence of enjoyment that can shape our life happiness.

Being happy _about_ our lives embraces all the things that make us happy _in_ our lives but is more holistic and all encompassing.

Martin Seligman is considered a pioneer of Positive Psychology, not simply because he has a systematic theory about why happy people are happy, but because he uses the scientific method to explore it. Seligman found that the most satisfied, upbeat people were those who had discovered and exploited their unique combination of "signature strengths", such as humanity, temperance, and persistence.

In his book, *Authentic Happiness*, Seligman writes that we can experience three kinds of happiness:

1. Pleasure and gratification.
2. Embodiment of strengths and virtues.
3. Meaning and purpose.

Each kind of happiness is linked to positive emotion. In his mind, there is progression from the first type of happiness of pleasure-and-gratification to strengths-and-virtues. What then follows is the sincerest form of happiness: meaning-and-purpose.

While we didn't specifically ask the question "What makes you most happy in life?" Women told us in so many words that happiness is tied to their physical and mental well-being.

Pleasure and gratification.

- ∞ While you're healthy, enjoy all your favorite activities.
- ∞ Meet amazing people.
- ∞ Time to take care of myself.
- ∞ How much I enjoy spending time with friends.
- ∞ Encountering a new world through travel.

Embodiment of strengths and virtues.

- ∞ Have strong interests, intellectual curiosity and good health. These are enormous positives.
- ∞ Stay curious, stay healthy and connect with others.
- ∞ Follow your interests, in particular learn new things and volunteer.

Meaning and purpose.

- ∞ Find a purpose that keeps you engaged and satisfied.
- ∞ The joy of volunteering.

You may find out that your happiness level changes as your journey moves from being in the thick-of-it to on my-own-terms, or out-of-the-paid-work-world. Ultimately, we discover that the end score doesn't really change, but the way we define happiness does.

Lists, lists and more lists

Some lists are good. They help us stay organized, give us a sense of purpose and help us plan for today and the future.

Lists can overwhelm us. To-do lists are task oriented. Bucket lists are the things or activities you'd like to do before you die. Reading lists contain books you'd like to read. DIY projects list interesting activities that you want to tackle yourself. How about password lists to help us remember all those darn passwords! Janet's calendar is her list. It goes everywhere with her and she'd be lost without it.

Let's face it, we all make lists, even mundane ones like grocery lists. Janice is worried that she is old fashioned because she still scratches down grocery items on a piece of paper instead of using her cell phone for notes.

Then there's the proverbial New Year's resolutions list. UGH. We usually equate this with changing our habits or adopting new ones. The most common resolutions include exercise more, lose weight, get organized, learn a new skill or hobby, live life to the fullest, save money, quit smoking, spend more time with family, on and on.

We don't know about you, but we tossed the New Year's resolution list out the window years ago. How many times do we need to tell ourselves, "I'm going to lose weight, or I'll work on eating a better diet, or I'm going to take better care of myself or I'll make a stronger effort to spend time with family and loved ones." Too many times to count.

Lists or no lists, we're smart enough to know what's important for our happiness, health and well-being, so let's just get on with it.

Pursuit of happiness

Research by Harvard Medical School has associated increased happiness with longevity and a lower risk of illness. The Harvard Study on Adult Development shows that 40% of people's happiness comes from the choices they make.

The researchers found that certain traits and behaviors are related with increased levels of happiness as we age. Two of the significant findings are "letting go" and "staying connected."

Letting go. The study shows that as we age, we tend to focus more on what's important to us, and we don't sweat the small stuff. We let go of matters that once seemed important but now appear trivial and not worth worrying about. We're better at leaving that stressful job or toxic relationship behind. We move more quickly away from our failures. We take stock of our lives, realize how short life is, and pay more attention to what makes us happy.

Thinking about "letting go", we asked women in the thick-of-it and on my-own-terms what aspects they would **NOT** miss in their career or professional lives.

There was agreement that three key things would NOT be missed:

1) Managing people and/or process.
2) Traveling for business.
3) Organized, scheduled, routines.

For women in the thick-of-it, there was near equal agreement that managing people and/or process and business travel would NOT be missed. These women are still highly involved in their careers and are not ready to change their relationship with the work-world.

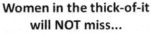

**Women in the thick-of-it
will NOT miss...**

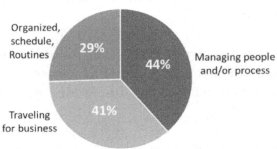

For women working on my-own-terms, business travel was the number-one thing they would NOT miss. Managing people and process dropped to number-three. These are women who have redefined themselves in the work-world; they have either started their own business or may not be working full-time. These women have already started "letting go" of the pressure of managing people and process because either they do not have people working for them or they set their own goals and how they are managed.

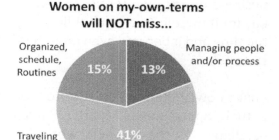

Women on my-own-terms will NOT miss...

Organized, schedule, Routines — 15%

Managing people and/or process — 13%

Traveling for business — 41%

Traveling for business ranked high for both groups of women as something they will NOT miss and will be happy to let go.

> *Janice's experience with business travel.*
> When I moved from my corporate career to working on my-own-terms as a consultant, the majority of my clients were not located "around the corner". I quickly found out that my business travel did not lessen at all, even though I was no longer in a full-time job where 60% of my time was spent traveling for business.
>
> My clients were either in Asia or the other side of North America. This was not really conducive to my new home which was on the west coast of Canada.

Yet, I really liked working on my-own-terms, and traveling for business was still required for me to deliver my work successfully.

The majority of my trips ended up being economy-class, because my clients were reluctant to pay for business-class travel. I was keen to run a profitable business on my-own-terms, so I was not willing to pay for it myself. As a result, I flew baggage-class all the time and it became even more burdensome and stressful.

I have now shifted my practice to more online and virtual opportunities, partly "thanks" to the pandemic. As the business world becomes more receptive to face-to-face client meetings, the need for business travel may be re-energized, but I am happy to leave it behind for the time being.

Staying connected. Keeping and developing strong relationships with family and friends brings us elements of joy and satisfaction. Regardless of where we are in relationship to the work-world, spending time with friends, spouses, partners, and family sits high on our enjoyment scale.

Thinking about your professional career, how important is networking to your success? Very! As professional women, we know that building strong business relationships can serve us well for career advancement, driving successful outcomes for our business, and stretching our knowledge in a multitude of ways. Our business relationships can even expand and develop into personal relationships that we foster into long-term friendships.

> *Janet and Janice's connection.*
> We met at a small start-up in Silicon Valley in the mid 90's. After both of us enjoyed a successful stint at that company, we left to pursue our own professional paths moving deeper into the thick-of-it, each in different high-profile directions. Janice moved to one of the top most valuable companies in the world. Janet joined a venture funded start-up for its debut, launch, and IPO (initial public offering). Over the years, we stayed in touch, although not regularly, but we still had the connection based on our professional time together.
>
> Then an impromptu breakfast meeting in Singapore reconnected us. Our friendship was rekindled after eighteen years. Janice was still intensely in the thick-of-it and Janet was working on my-own-terms.
>
> Shortly thereafter Janice stepped out of the thick-of-it and started working on my-own-terms. Our friendship and relationship thrive today with 1700 km (1000 miles) between us and we find ourselves as co-authors of this book. Through this process we have discovered new things about each other and realized how much in common we share.

In a Harvard study, Dr. Robert Waldinger, states that "personal connection creates mental and emotional stimulation, which are automatic mood boosters."

We heard from many women how important it is to stay connected.

- ∞ Stay curious, stay healthy and connect with others.
- ∞ Keep busy. Be open to new friendships. Surround yourself with people in similar circumstances.
- ∞ Essential to stay engaged with the world and maintain a strong sense of social relationships and a sense of community.

How do you stay connected? Sometimes it takes an unprecedented situation that makes us realize the importance of being connected. Perhaps it's a personal life changing event like losing someone close to us, or even something like the global pandemic that gave us opportunities through technology to engage and rekindle relationships.

Connection
*The energy that exists between people
when they feel seen, heard, and valued;
when they can give and receive without judgment;
and when they derive sustenance and strength
from the relationship.*
Brené Brown, Professor, Author

Staying connected takes effort. For some of us, it comes easy, and we make it a part of our daily action. Others may have to make a conscious effort depending on the type of engagement, such as community involvement, or keeping those Sunday night family gatherings alive! Figure out what works for you.

Wellness and its impact to our health

---

*Wellness is a state of complete physical, mental,
and social well-being,
not merely the absence of disease or infirmity.*
The World Health Organization (WHO)

Wellness is an ongoing process of making the right choices towards a healthy and fulfilling life. It is especially important because taking care of ourselves physically and mentally will help prevent ailments that can plague us in the future.

In researching this topic, we found multiple definitions of wellness. The Global Wellness Institute, a non-profit organization, defines wellness as the active pursuit of activities, choices, and lifestyles that lead to a state of holistic health.

There are two important aspects to this definition. First, wellness is not a passive or static state but rather an active pursuit that is associated with intentions, choices and actions as we work toward an optimal state of health and well-being. Second, wellness is linked to holistic health— it extends beyond physical health and incorporates many different dimensions that should work in harmony.

Wellness not only pertains to our physical state of health, but it also encompasses our social, intellectual and emotional well-being.

This is the Global Wellness Institute's succinct summary of multi-dimensional wellness.

- **Physical:** A healing body through exercise, nutrition, sleep, etc.
- **Mental:** Engagement with the world through learning, problem-solving, creativity, etc.
- **Emotional:** Being in touch with, aware of, accepting of, and able to express one's feelings (and those of others).
- **Spiritual:** Our search for meaning and purpose in human existence.
- **Social:** Connecting with, interacting with, and contributing to other people and our communities.
- **Environmental:** A healthy physical environment free of hazards; awareness of the role we play in bettering rather than denigrating the natural environment.

In comparison, the National Institute of Wellness applies a similar six-dimensional approach using occupational, in lieu of environmental, as one of its six segments. The occupational dimension is one that we resonate with because it recognizes the personal satisfaction and enrichment in life through work.

Wellness was echoed by many women. Here is what they had to say and how they practice it.

Women in the thick-of-it have a clear wellness plan.

∞ I am a strong believer in maintaining an active mind and lifestyle to live a long and happy life. I've seen too many people die not long after leaving the paid work-world. Working, whether for income or otherwise, facilitates having purpose, staying focused and continuing to achieve life goals.

∞ A few important things that I will keep in mind when I move to my next relationship with the work-world:
  o Keep engaged with friends and family.
  o Have young friends.
  o Keep fit.
  o Always have activities planned out in the future.
  o Get involved in activities that keep your mind active.
  o Don't think of yourself as being old.

∞ Leaving the paid work-world is not a hard and fast fact … it is a progression into the next great thing! If done properly, you can realize your inner desires and aspirations you didn't have time for during the earning years.

∞ My intention is to work until I get to my early sixties. I have the energy to straddle both aspects of my world: corporate life and ranch life. Until something changes, I'll figure it out to the best of my ability, with whatever resources I may need.

Women working on my-own-terms plan, ponder, and are concerned about future wellness.

∞ Yes, there is uncertainty that lies ahead. I wonder… as I age, will I have a level of mental and physical health that allows me to fully enjoy life, as I have come to expect? Will I continue to have a fulfilling life that includes interesting adventures, connecting with wonderful people, and fun? In recent years, I have seen the passing of dear friends and thus mortality has become much more real for me.

∞ Stave off dementia. I worry that leaving the paid work-world will accelerate my potential for dementia. My father had Alzheimer's.

∞ I relish the opportunity to spend time with a more diverse and more creative set of individuals after leaving the corporate scene.

Women out-of-the-paid-work-world remain engaged for optimal wellness.

∞ While I have left paid employment, I have not left working for the greater good. I find my skills are very much appreciated in the non-profit world.

∞ Everyone chooses their own lane. It is essential to stay engaged with the world and maintain strong social relationships and a sense of community. Staying healthy is a big one for me in order to have the ability to keep pursuing new opportunities and adventures. Being bored is not an option.

∞ Having strong interests, intellectual curiosity and good health are enormous positives.

∞ I would recommend "retiring" as soon as it is financially possible. We only have a window of time before our bodies and brains give out. Travel as much as possible. Exercise daily. Eat healthy. Entertain. Nourish friendships and relationships with your family.

Mary G is following her bliss and gifts.
After fifteen high-powered years as a leader in various customer facing roles in the high-tech industry, I decided to put my career on 'pause' and focus my time on raising my two sons. Admittedly, I realized that I wasn't ready to leave the career world just yet, and after some reflection while hiking in the woods of California, I started to explore part-time work.

Serendipity struck when Janet called and asked me if I would be interested in doing a consulting project. I jumped at the opportunity. We discovered that our unique set of skills could be packaged and then along with my husband, we co-founded KickStart Alliance. I found myself back in the thick-of-it, knee deep in marketing and sales consultancy projects.

Eighteen years flew by. I enjoyed working on projects that offered me continuous learning experiences and most important, flexibility. Flexibility to pursue my interests in spirituality, songwriting, plant-based nutrition, organic gardening and environmentalism. I was finally at a point in my career and life to be able to do things that brought me satisfaction. This meant being able to work on my-own-terms, with the freedom to build upon my interests that can benefit others who seek better health and well-being. What more could I ask for?

Armed with a certificate in plant-based nutrition from the T. Colin Campbell Center for Nutrition Studies, I partnered with my sister-in-law and

created   www.plant-based4health.com.   It   is
tremendously satisfying to be able to help people
who are curious about adopting a plant-based
lifestyle and the healthful beneficial impact it brings
to their lives!

I didn't stop there. Two years later, I co-founded
Soul Healing Studio offering spiritual coaching and
meditation classes (www.soulhealingstudio.com). I
am now even busier than ever. A busyness that
brought me happiness, doing things and helping
others through my lifelong interests.

Music and songwriting have always been my
creative passion and after sharing one of my songs
with a friend, I found myself invited to a jam session,
that ultimately turned into the formation of a rock
cover band! I stretched my wings as lead singer and
guitarist, realizing that I found my true calling as a
performer.

It was time to finally leave my consulting 'work'
behind. I was burned out. I began to spend time on
my music and the direction I wanted to take with it.
I knew there was something out there for me.

Fast forward one more year. Through a mutual
friend, I met a multi-instrumentalist and producer.
We got right to work on an album of my original New
Age / Pop songs encompassing positivity, peace,
spirituality, and well-being. It's my dream come
true. My first album, *Time to Soar*, was the perfect
title, now on to the second album, *People Passing*

Through (www.thesonggardeners.com). I look forward to discovering what comes next.

I've learned much about myself. I am approaching my life passions (my bliss) with the talents (and gifts) I am blessed with and doing it all on my-own-terms!

healthy body + healthy mind = happy life

The many facets of healthcare

Healthcare is a difficult topic and we struggle with it. On one hand, it should be straightforward. On the other, it presents complexity, is multi-dimensional, and is interpreted in many different ways – depending on where we live, our health condition, or the state of our current health system.

Merriam-Webster defines healthcare as the efforts made to maintain or restore physical, mental, or emotional well-being especially by trained and licensed professionals. In today's world, healthcare encompasses any service, organization, and means for taking care of your health.

The World Health Organization (WHO) characterises **primary** healthcare as a whole society approach to health and well-being centered on the needs and preferences of individuals, families, and communities.

WHO states that primary healthcare should provide whole-person care for physical, mental, and social health and well-being. The health needs are for the whole person throughout their lifespan, not just for a set of specific diseases. A primary healthcare approach ensures people receive comprehensive care – ranging from prevention to treatment, rehabilitation to palliative care – as close as is feasible to their everyday environment.

Depending where we live, our options for well managed healthcare can differ dramatically. Our healthcare concerns are amplified as we move between being in the thick-of-it, on my-own-terms, and out-of-the-paid-work-world. This is especially true if our financial foundation is not strong enough to address unforeseen health concerns or where local healthcare is under resourced.

As we consider what's important to us in healthcare, we mentally make a list of our must-haves and important-to-haves. This list will be dynamic depending on where we are in relation to the work-world.

Other variables include our current state of health, where we live and our individual or dependent status. We may find that the important-to-have in the table below, shifts to the must-have, depending on our circumstances. Our personal health status may change, or our relationship to the work world may change, requiring us to reevaluate what's necessary.

Here is an example of what a healthcare priority chart may look like. Yours will look different.

Must-have	Important-to-have
Access & location to healthcare providers	Affordability of services (insurance)
Reputable specialist care	Wellness / preventative
Emergency treatment	Vision
Non-elective surgery	Palliative care when needed
Dentistry	Massage therapy

An "ideal" healthcare system

Is there such a thing as the perfect or ideal healthcare system? An article titled *Judging Health Systems: Focusing on What Matters* appeared in a Harvard Chan School of Public Health post. We agree with the author's viewpoint that most people want a healthcare system where they can get timely access to high quality, affordable care and one that promotes innovation of new tests and treatments.

Beyond access to a quality healthcare system, we want care that we can afford. We know that services come at a cost and those services that support a primary healthcare approach differ vastly based on where we live or how we choose to manage our own lifestyle.

Is one place better than the other? Do we make choices on where to live based on the affordability or access to healthcare services?

> *Janice's experience with various healthcare systems.* During my professional career, I had the opportunity to live in three countries. My experiences with

healthcare systems varied. In my very early career, I was indifferent regarding healthcare. I was naïve, thinking nothing could happen to me, and besides I was living in Canada, whose medical system "took care" of us.

As I settled into a new life in California, it became very apparent that working for an employer who offered health insurance was a benefit not to be underestimated. Fortunately for me and my family, we did not encounter any serious health issues outside of the preventative healthcare measures we practiced. Needless to say, we made sure we had the right coverage in the event something happened. Even so, supplemental insurance premiums were costly, despite the fact that my employer subsidized a sizable portion.

Fast forward to my career move to Singapore. Although I continued having healthcare benefits from my employer, our experience with the healthcare system was tested during our 14+ years there. From surgeries to concussions to SARS-CoV (Severe Acute Respiratory Syndrome - Coronavirus), we experienced a quality level of healthcare unmatched to what we had in the past.

We knew at some point we would leave Singapore. It became clear to us that having affordable healthcare and quality services was a critical factor in determining our next location.

I consider myself fortunate, being Canadian, we could include Canada as a choice for our next location. And that's what we did.

Does Canada have the "ideal" healthcare system? Many would argue, not necessarily so. For now, it is serving my family well. We have tested the system rigorously and, so far, it has held up to the positive side of its reputation.

Regardless of where we choose to live, many of us need some type of insurance that would pay for routine or unexpected healthcare expenses. We may find that our single-payer or Medicare insurance doesn't cover wellness checks, dentistry, elective (but needed) surgeries, or out-of-country travel. As we enjoy more flexibility to travel, we recognize that travel insurance plays a more critical role and gives us peace of mind should the unthinkable happen.

In economic theory, as well as the lay opinion, whatever goods and services are provided, they must be paid for by someone. You don't get something for nothing. And so, it is with healthcare.

Top of mind concerns

Women who responded to our survey, regardless of their relationship to the work-world, overwhelmingly stated that the number-one thing they worry about is an unforeseen emergency situation that may impact them personally or financially.

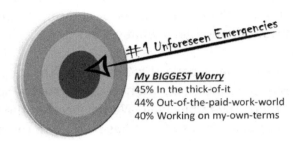

My BIGGEST Worry
45% In the thick-of-it
44% Out-of-the-paid-work-world
40% Working on my-own-terms

The next two areas of concern included personal health and that of our families, and not having health insurance coverage for ample healthcare choices.

My next BIG worries

40% Out-of-paid-work-world
29% In the thick-of-it
24% On my-own-terms

24% In the thick-of-it
24% On my-own-terms
17% Out-of-paid-work-world

According to Reuters Health and the Journal of American Medical Association, nearly half of Americans aged 50 to 64 worry they won't be able to afford healthcare when they retire, and more than two-thirds are concerned that federal policy changes will affect their current health insurance.

Ostensibly, this may not be relevant for those who have the opportunity to live in a single-payer healthcare system. Even so, our degree and ability to have health coverage regardless of where we choose to live may depend on the type of services that are necessary for our own personal situation.

Healthcare – navigating the unknown

The cost is unpredictable and uncontrollable.

- ∞ Retirement at 65 doesn't work anymore. It worked when people didn't live as long and working to age 65 was a lifelong job. I worry about having enough savings and income, particularly when health is a concern or problem.
- ∞ Healthcare is the only thing that stops me from leaving my paid career. If I could figure out a healthcare solution that gives me accessibility to the right providers when and how I need it, then it lessens the barrier. I've been twice diagnosed with thyroid cancer. Until healthcare is more settled for me, it holds me back.
- ∞ I really didn't take the time to think about medical issues and what I should have known in advance of leaving paid employment.
- ∞ My concerns are more about keeping healthy and as I "advance", where I will need to live – location, type of facility, and cost. The term "advance" was what my late mother used; she lived to the age of 98.
- ∞ I could leave the paid work-world, but we need the health insurance.

Juanita T's lifelong career.
I started my nursing career forty-six years ago, and I guess you could say I haven't really stopped. My

journey began as a pediatric nurse in Montreal, Canada. Originally, I wanted to be a physician, so during my early days in school I volunteered in the pediatric ward. It was obvious to me that nurses were the true caregivers, and that changed my mind to shift from a career in medicine to nursing.

When the government decided to centralize pediatric care to specialized hospitals, I decided to adapt and learn new skills as a critical care nurse. I never looked back, and spent the next thirty-nine years in the Intensive Care Unit in one of the best recognized acute care hospitals in Canada.

As a healthcare professional, the benefits and disadvantages in our healthcare system seemed clear. The approach "healthcare for all" regardless of income, background, ethnicity, age or health status is touted as a perfect system. It's a system that's supposed to take away the "worry" of not being able to afford quality healthcare.

What doesn't work, or at least what I've seen, is accessibility. Accessibility to healthcare providers – doctors, specialists and general practitioners (GPs) – can be severely limited depending on the urban or rural area where we live.

One would think that being a nurse, I would have access to my network of references and contacts in the healthcare system. Not necessarily so. At one point, I was even put on an "orphan list" for people who didn't have a GP. The only option in the meantime, was to rely on walk-in clinics or emergency departments for care.

Even with a single-payer system such as we have here in Canada, many of us opt for private health insurance, a costly but not outrageous alternative. It gives us better accessibility and can lower our wait times substantially. Like having my knee replaced and not having to wait two years!

Aside from paying out-of-pocket for private healthcare, I see technology playing a good role in addressing accessibility. COVID-19 was a game changer in this field, with Telemedicine getting a significant foothold as an alternative for non-critical healthcare support. I hope to see Telemedicine gather greater adoption which could help alleviate some of the chokehold on accessibility, and not just be a "nice to have".

I recognize that a very big part of who I am is being a lifelong nurse. Thinking about my own retirement, at the age of fifty I went back to university to earn my BSc in Nursing, which ultimately gave me a better pension and put me on a higher pay scale. It also gave me the option to continue in other fields of care should I decide to do so.

After forty-six years, I took the plunge and left my job at the hospital. It enabled me to take care of my mom, who sadly died the year I retired. Emotionally I was not ready to leave the paid work-world. I was still grieving; I was no longer working in a capacity where I could take care of people. I felt I was outside a room looking in, when it should have been me taking care of that patient.

In the meantime, I started doing volunteer work at our local palliative care facility, working in their gardens in the summer. It was one of my lifelong goals to work in palliative care – and pretty soon, I graduated from gardening duties to a palliative care nurse at the facility!

After forty-six years of being in the thick-of-it, now I am working on my-own-terms. I don't think I'll ever truly retire. Through my work in palliative care, I learned that dying well is just as important as living well.

Our health check

In thinking about our own state of health, we asked all the women in our survey to assess their current health status, taking into consideration a combination of exercise, nutrition, stress, and sleep.

The good news is that we are <u>really</u> taking care of ourselves! Nearly half of us responded that our current health status is "very good", and one-third stated their health is "excellent". Almost one-fifth of us are relatively good, and a small percentage rate themselves as average or below.

Thinking about the following chart, more than ninety-percent of us believe that our health assessment measures above average, from relatively good to excellent. Being healthy is a happy state!

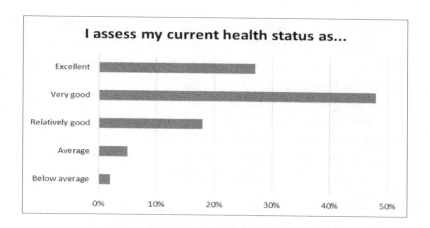

Over ninety percent of our respondents fall between the ages of 50 to 70+, with the majority being in the age group of 50 to 69. WOW! Professional women clearly put health as a priority in their lifestyle.

> *When women take care of their health*
> *they become their own best friend.*
> Maya Angelou
> American Poet, Author, Civil Rights Activist

A full life

Live life to the fullest! We've all heard that, and even said it. What does it mean to live a full life?

Living a full life is about continually reaching out for newer, enriching experiences that propel our personal growth and push our boundaries to better ourselves and help others along the way.

Yet, our definition of living a full-life changes as our life progresses. We re-examine our goals. Our perspective changes as our longevity increases. We want those increased years to count because it's the only life we have.

> *I don't want to get to the end of my life*
> *and find that I have just lived the length of it.*
> *I want to have lived the width of it as well.*
> Diane Ackerman
> American Poet, Author, Essayist and Naturalist

In *Chapter 2: Voices of the Age of Freedom*, you heard the women in our survey describe themselves. We are women who see freedom to explore new ideas and interests, choice, transformation, action, independence, and invention. We are on our way to living life to the fullest, if we are not already there!

In this chapter, we have explored happiness, wellness and healthcare. Each of these has a place in our lives. They may be more or less pronounced depending where we are in our life journey and what obstacles have been thrown our way.

Happiness is a key component to living a full life. We set about doing things that are important to us and make us happy. We plan and set goals that endeavor to keep ourselves engaged and passionate in our pursuits. We know that happiness is tied to our physical and mental well-being.

Wellness is an active pursuit. It is linked with choices and actions that lead us towards achieving an ideal state of health and well-being. This takes practice, and for some of us it takes extra conscious effort. Being resilient, having the ability to bounce back, having a positive outlook, and doing acts of kindness are a few ways we build on our well-being.

Healthcare is something both internal and external. Internal healthcare is how we take care of ourselves — what we do, eat, exercise, and surround ourselves with. External healthcare is what's available to us through government, insurance, and private services. With both, our choices to pursue options contribute to living life to its fullest.

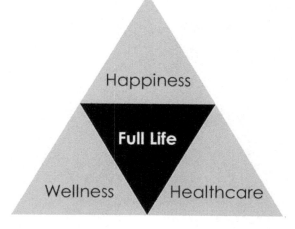

We want to savor life's pleasures and live life to the fullest. We are committed to life goals and ambitions we set for ourselves. There is also a health conundrum that we face, because physical health is intrinsic to living fully.

Practicing a full life requires consistency, equilibrium, and the willingness to sacrifice some things along the way. We may find that we can practice some things more easily than others. That's OK. Afterall, we are complex individuals living in a complex world.

Chapter 5

Reflecting on the Impact of a Global Pandemic

When we first embarked on our book project, COVID-19 was unknown and the pandemic that ensued was nowhere in our minds.

In consideration of the pandemic, we returned to the women of our survey and asked how it affected their lives. Whether we find ourselves in the thick-of-it, working on my-own-terms, or out-of-the-paid-work-world, the pandemic changed the way we work, live, and play.

Our lives changed dramatically. We lost friends, family members, and loved ones. We suffered through the pain of knowing someone who endured this terrible disease. Amidst all of that, we discovered that our lives have been intrinsically changed forever.

In looking back at SARS-CoV and the COVID-19 pandemic, we notice a correlation. SARS-CoV is a contraction for the formal name of that past virus, **S**evere **A**cute **R**espiratory **S**yndrome - **Co**rona**V**irus. COVID-19 is a contraction for the official name of the more current virus, **CO**rona**VI**rus **D**isease – 20**19**. The CDC (Centers for Disease Control) tells us that the virus causing COVID-19 is not the same as the Coronaviruses that commonly circulate among humans and cause mild illness, like the common cold. Thinking about the future, we don't know if we will see another Coronavirus, but we are now aware that viruses can dramatically affect us globally.

> *Janice has first-hand experience.*
> The COVID-19 pandemic makes me reflect on my time living in Singapore during the 2003 SARS-CoV outbreak. Within a period of five to six months, the disease infected 8,000 people in more than twenty-five countries and left over 800 dead. The majority were in China and Hong Kong, but Canada and Singapore suffered as well, being fourth and fifth of the most exposed and number of deaths. Certainly, the outbreak did not have anywhere near the scale or global impact as COVID-19, but it was still a terrible disease to contend with.
>
> During this time, the country of Singapore was quarantined. The borders were only lifted after thirty days had passed with no new cases reported. We struggled for two months, waiting for controls to be lifted and more importantly for the disease to be eliminated. It was a scary time for me and my family.

Similar to what we experienced with the global pandemic, masks and sanitizer were hard to find. Temperature checks were mandatory in all public places and a rigorous health program was put in place to educate people on the importance of washing your hands and isolation when necessary. Sound familiar?

Fast forward eighteen years, I realize how lucky we were that SARS in Singapore never hit the magnitude of human loss or tragedy that COVID-19 has introduced. Our youngest son was twelve years old at the time of the SARS outbreak and to this day, handwashing continues to be a part of his diligence in protecting his health. A simple behavior such as handwashing, became a tipping point needed to help combat this insidious disease.

Each of us has our own stories and insight on how the pandemic has impacted us. It's such a pivotal topic. We returned to the women who responded to our original survey and asked about the impact COVID-19 had on the ways they work and live. Some of the changes will be short lived and other changes will stay with us. Here is what they had to say:

- ∞ It changed how I work.
- ∞ My health, well-being and happiness suffered.
- ∞ I'm adapting.
- ∞ It has affected family and friends.
- ∞ Social routines have been lost and disrupted.
- ∞ Government has a big impact.

How work changed due to COVID-19

Covid-19 changed the way we work in numerous ways: unexpected furloughs, forced part-time, remote working, home schooling and even early retirement. Technology became a vital resource, whether we liked it or not.

The impact was hard, fast and undesirable

Working from home (WFH) negatively impacted my business and my company.

∞ Professionally, education has taken a hit. My business is down about 30-40%. My biggest clients are private schools with international boarding students and many of them did not return. Secondly, many families lost their jobs and tutoring is a luxury that has to wait. Third, there's been so much confusion and change in the way a school functions, this has affected day-to-day activities. It's been a slow re-start.

∞ Sales is challenging. It is hard to reach potential clients since they aren't working from an office with a phone, companies aren't spending money, CFOs are trying to make payroll, and don't want to spend money on new projects. We are tired of Zoom calls.

∞ Being self-employed with no salary and being the sole bread winner, my business was adversely affected by COVID-19. My husband was laid off before COVID-19 and once the real impact of the pandemic hit, it has been near impossible for him to find an opportunity. The impact was immediate but we are doing better now.

The downside to WFH is the absence of social and business physical connections.

∞ COVID-19 forced my company to have employees work from home. I miss the informal interactions of the office. It's hard to reach people with WFH. I don't have a sense what others are working on, how busy they are, or when is a good time to reach them.

∞ We now run our business on Zoom meetings and have few in-person meetings. As a short-term remedy that's fine, but not being able to meet with colleagues and associates is not sustainable in the long-term for innovation and growth.

∞ For a couple of years, I had the best of both worlds. I volunteered in the classroom as often as I preferred, then went home and did "retired people" stuff. I really miss working with children and supporting the classroom teacher. Providing online support for the classroom is extremely limiting. It is frustrating being unable to do an effective job.

∞ Broadly speaking, I think we are operating on a reservoir of "social capital" in terms of connection to our colleagues and clients. I worry what will happen when this runs dry. How do we replenish the connections virtually? That being said, Zoom is actually better for establishing relationships initially, better than by phone ... so there's that!

Job opportunities evaporated when the pandemic hit.

∞ I started an amazing new job just days before the pandemic took hold, only to be let go four months later due to COVID-19. I found another job four months after that, but had to take on more risk, working for close to 100% commission. Many of my friends who were established at companies were not let go; being a new hire a few days before COVID-19 was bad timing.

∞ Early in the pandemic I connected with a psychologist who I use to work with and offered to volunteer for her organization doing workplace health coaching. She was keen to have me join her team, and I went through all of the hoops to get on board. Unfortunately, the project that she had intended for me fell through due to lack of funding. I was disappointed that the project did not pan out as I was quite jazzed about doing it. It made me realize that I miss doing substantive work.

∞ I am a professional symphonic musician and on the Board of a professional orchestra. Our season's orchestra performances have all been canceled.

Some things haven't changed

For women already working from home the changes were minor.

∞ Not a ton has changed. I've worked from home for nineteen years.

∞ There was a bit of an adjustment. I set some boundaries so that I wouldn't get the formerly welcome "pop ins" of neighbors stopping by or calling me during my work hours. Fortunately, COVID-19 hasn't changed the way I work or live, because I had been a remote worker for nearly ten years so I was set up to do the same. I'll never go back to an office, unless it's traveling to a customer's site.

∞ The pandemic has not changed the way we work or live for the most part. But now we cook every night, we see friends much less often and only one or two at a time, only outdoors, and we don't really go anywhere.

Some things have improved for the better

The pandemic made WFH more acceptable.

∞ Professionally, I've always worked from home and I have adapted to meetings and interviewing by video conference and LOVE IT! My tutors have adapted to teaching online and they LOVE IT. I am a bit concerned they won't want to go back to in-person teaching again. But I will deal with that when the time comes.

∞ I am only now realizing what a good move it was twenty years ago to make a switch to a more portable career. I did this pretty much intentionally and it has paid off, way more than I expected.

WFH has turned out to be a blessing.

∞ I am grateful, I really enjoy what I do! The biggest impact the pandemic is having on me personally is working remotely and supporting many clients 100% virtually. Other than Zoom fatigue, it has gone well!

∞ I have to admit that as I get older, now 73, and have less energy than I used to have, working from home has been a blessing.

∞ I feel really guilty about this, but it's been a Godsend for me. In the context of breaking the traditional requirement of having to BE in the office, the pandemic turned it upside down. It created a new way to communicate. It's helped me manage my time better. I start my day at 6AM and work until 4PM. Then I am free to work on our ranch in the evenings and weekends. While there was initial stress to cope with the new work style, it alleviated the commute stress and gave back time.

WFH saves me time and money. There are more remote worker options.

∞ I don't miss my commute and I have been surprised by how much I enjoy working from home.

∞ The pandemic introduced new business models that will thrive. Video and collaboration have become the norm.

∞ I am a serial networker, which is important to my business. In-person events have been replaced by online events, so this has changed how I expand my network in a positive way.

∞ I have been a freelance career coach for over three years now. COVID-19 has actually helped my work situation because it is now even more "acceptable" to coach online or coach in-person at my home. I used to pay for office space at a business center for private coaching sessions.

WFH added positive changes to the way my company and our teams work.

∞ I started "The Gift of Time" on Fridays for my team. Fridays are reserved for getting our work done (no meetings) and catching up from all the meetings we've had. Surprisingly, the accomplishments we got done in the year of COVID-19 was remarkable. It really drove empowerment to the team.

∞ My company and I became more focused in what we can do for the community. We are doing pro bono work for non-profits and small businesses to help them survive, thrive, and accomplish their missions.

∞ As a healthcare professional, I have less laundry as I no longer wear my personal uniform. My employer now provides scrubs as an infection prevention measure. I do wear PPE (personal protection equipment) for every patient I x-ray: medical mask, gloves, eye protection, and gown for contact and droplet precautions. What we gain in shortening the exam time is offset by the post exam cleaning process. I also live in a community where I feel completely safe on the job. Bonus!

The composition of work changed

COVID-19 introduced new ways to manage work routines. In some cases, it accelerated work decisions that would likely not have been considered before the pandemic. Many women were open to take on more risks and explore other avenues that they would never have dreamed of doing before. Like listening to a musical composition, some women turned the volume up, some turned the volume down, and some changed to listen to something entirely new.

New opportunities emerged that had some women "turn up the volume" of work.

∞ The biggest impact is that it's driven me back to full-time work. I was laid off in 2016 from a large software company and was hired back as a contractor. I'd been working part-time on my-own-terms until the beginning of the pandemic. The implementation work that I was doing dried up as the company's customers canceled or postponed projects. I decided to reach out to an old boss. He found a position within his organization and I made the leap back into Silicon Valley full-time start-up life again.

∞ Working from home encourages me. My energy may last longer than I previously thought. I may be able to continue working full-time longer. So, my timeline to working on my-own-terms has shifted. Others I work with are sharing similar insights and thoughts.

∞ I believe this new generation of women leaders is doing great things and I am learning from working with them. I now work with a small women-owned company which has given me new inspiration. Our company is still building and has been impacted, but the whole thing has been a welcome surprise. We have found ways to work outside in-person when the weather allows. When winter arrived, work was mostly virtual which felt like a new loss.

∞ My professional background includes my experience as a psychologist. I recently reached out to a colleague with the same background to talk about what I'd like to do next. In some ways, the pandemic has helped because it gives you tons of opportunities to think about, as well as what's really important and what's not.

Some women "turned down the volume" of work to either work on my-own-terms or step out-of-the-paid-work-world.

∞ My long-term contract was not renewed and so I decided to mostly step out-of-the-paid-work-world, which I am enjoying tremendously. I can spend time with the people I love and do what I enjoy doing. I am doing more project work and I'm blessed that I have work coming to me without doing much marketing.

∞ I am figuring out my career transition and made a list of my values and ideas. I'm looking at being a HICAP volunteer; the Health Insurance Counseling & Advocacy Program helping people choose and select the best Medicare plan for them. I'm looking at Sierra Club volunteering. I will spend more time investing my money and growing my savings. I look forward to less stress and less daily career demands but I expect there will be less intellectual challenge as well.

∞ I took on a couple of short work projects during the first several months of the pandemic that I hadn't planned on. I had begun to step out-of-the-paid-work-world prior to this and those six to seven months served as a good "dress rehearsal" for the pandemic. I got used to a slower pace, not traveling for work, and being home with my husband 24/7. I learned about Zoom calls; they are fun and easy!

∞ Even though I retired from teaching in the classroom, I still keep up with the latest educational programs and philosophies as a Senior Volunteer in local schools. This program was put on hold due to schools using online classroom instruction. I still plan to do some private face-to-face tutoring once the coast is clear.

Health, well-being, and happiness

If our health and well-being wasn't already top-of-mind, suddenly COVID-19 brought it to the forefront. It made us more vulnerable, if not for ourselves, certainly for elderly relations, parents, siblings, aunts, uncles, and friends. We became acutely aware of what was happening around us. Our emotional state took a toll. For some of us, social media was overwhelming. For others, it was an avenue to reconnect and rekindle lost relationships.

On the positive side, some of us shifted focus and activities centered around home improvement, upping our health, cooking at home, and reconnecting with friends and family. We found things to be grateful for.

We realize that's it's okay NOT to be in control and "go with the flow."

∞ I'm less stressed about work since I can't do much to change the crisis, so I'm way more relaxed about business. I love not being able to shop. I never liked malls or shopping anyway. I support local businesses and order from meal prep companies. And I'm still baking sourdough!!

∞ I talk on the phone more to family and friends. I do have to make a real effort to keep in touch. I'm taking it one day at a time. I am learning about being in the moment more and more.

∞ Patience is key. I'm Jewish so I can say this, the Anne Frank rule applies here: the only thing that matters is surviving until the end. If we don't make it until the "All Clear", it's a failure, no matter how close we get. We are taking no chances and being very, very risk-averse. I keep my grandparents in mind, who survived World War II, because while our generation may find self-sacrifice unfamiliar, it's really not.

∞ I miss being surrounded by a "normal" world where people talk about things other than COVID-19. But I have been interested to watch the acceleration of many changes that would have taken much longer, if not for it.

∞ We have not set foot in any commercial building since March 2020. We closed the purchase of our new home signing documents on the hood of our car outside the closing attorney's office. We use Instacart for the delivery of all of our groceries. We are watching movies at home instead of going out for dinner or to the theatre. We have postponed travel until the vaccine is widely available and the pandemic has subsided. We exercise at home rather than at the gym and spend as much time walking outdoors as possible.

It deepened our sense of gratitude.

∞ I feel fortunate and blessed. I feel privileged to call New Zealand home. I feel that I have been cared for by my friends, my employer, and my government. For those still locked down and at risk, a day does not go by without me thinking of you and wishing that soon you too will be bathed in sunshine and happiness.

∞ I am more mindful of what I have. I am less materialistic. I have made time to help others. I have walked away from the pressure often felt by spending too much time on social media. I may have a few more kilos than last year, but they are healthy kilos from spending more time outside and exercising.

∞ The pandemic has taught me to be more patient and grateful for what both my husband and I have – our health, food on our table, a comfortable home, good friends and supportive family members. It has taught me to rethink my priorities and to slow down and enjoy small moments in life. Some call this "mindfulness" which I think is an apt term. I am also optimistic about the future and know that the pandemic will pass. My wish is that society will learn some invaluable lessons about tolerance, caring for self and others, as well as the environment. I like to think the virus has been a bit of wake-up call.

On the discouraging side, the pandemic brought adverse conditions to many and impacted their well-being. Anxiety and anxiousness mounted as concern for self, family, and friends grew. Things we enjoyed were impacted by a situation we couldn't control. Proactive health plans were curtailed. For some, COVID-19 brought out the dragons which had been hidden from view.

∞ The pandemic showed me that I default to working my way through something at the expense of other things, like my health. While I had months to determine a new routine with the change of schedule, for several months I worked longer days with fewer breaks until I realized this was not a good strategy long-term.

∞ Our life shut down completely with the pandemic. I'm only fifty-five but my husband is sixty-eight, so he's at higher risk. We haven't been in a grocery store. We don't go anywhere or do anything, and don't plan to until it's safe - very safe - to do so.

∞ Oh, and then there is my waistline. That certainly has changed, and not for the better.

∞ Constant fear. Fear for my own health, my husband's health, and my adult children's health. Fear about the planet and humanity. Fear about possible financial instability. Just a constant and inescapable fear.

∞ My anxiety level has increased with regards to people not following public health guidelines and people who do not believe in science.

Making the best of it.

∞ I found myself shouting at the TV, frustrated with social media, reaching for the gin more often and even contemplating ripping up my passport from the country of my birth. My solution: limit news to one hour per day, remove myself almost completely from social media, and focus on helping others in small ways.

∞ I'm somewhat depressed with the pandemic; it has severely limited my ability to travel the world. I'm making the best of it and bought a national park pass for me and my son. We are hitting the road whenever we can to see the parks of the U.S.

∞ Not seeing friends and family takes a toll for sure. I do a few things differently now. I spend more time in my kitchen learning new recipes. I've committed to volunteering again after a six-year hiatus because I was "too busy!" I don't go anywhere other than the grocery store. I wear a mask wherever I go. I spend less money. So all-in-all, it's not so bad.

Keeping busy improves a positive outlook.

∞ Home improvement was a theme during the pandemic. I redecorated a few rooms in my house. I installed solar panels on my house. Since it's so hot and sunny where I live, it was positive to harness the sun and reduce ever increasing power bills.

∞ Our life continues with exercise, walking the dog, and I'm getting tons done around the house. I've reorganized and cleaned out every closet and drawer in the house. If this pandemic ended tomorrow, my big question is: What would I be most sorry for not getting done while I had the opportunity?

∞ It's easier to stay active, walking every day, than coming home exhausted after a long commute.

How we adapted

Life handed him a lemon,
As Life sometimes will do.
His friends looked on in pity,
Assuming he was through.
They came upon him later,
Reclining in the shade
In calm contentment,
Drinking a glass of lemonade.
Clarence Edwin Flynn - 1940 - "The Optimist"

Our lifestyles changed. Those activities we took for granted now needed a different approach.

Simple activities like going to the grocery store or running mundane errands now took planning. Our home kitchens became the focal point of our daily lives. For some of us, it was a joy, for others a chore. We needed to adapt to a new way of sustaining ourselves. Our pleasure in eating out became replaced with the creation of new meals. Who would have thought that baking powder or yeast would become hard to find! And toilet paper? Let's not go there...

Zoom, the internet, cooking and online streaming to the rescue!

- ∞ My writer's club meets by Zoom, so do other organizations I participate in. Actually, I prefer this. I don't have to drive to get there and can participate in my PJs.
- ∞ Because I can't see friends for happy hour and dinners, I'm watching MUCH more television. Thank God for Netflix, Amazon Prime, HBO and Hulu.
- ∞ I cook about 70% more than before. Yes, we still get meals to-go from restaurants, but not anywhere near the rate pre-COVID-19. I now prefer eating at home, not wasting time in restaurants.
- ∞ I still pursue some of my hobbies, particularly music and learning. I am grateful for technology (like the internet and Zoom) which provide many opportunities to explore new interests through online courses in art, language, history, and more.

Reprioritizing what's important.

∞ I have used the time to work on my 40-year TO-DO list. Many of the things on the list are solitary tasks, like closet organization, which take MUCH more time than anyone realizes. I hope to not look on the pandemic as a lost year, but as a time of checking-off a lot of personal TO-DOs, so I am ready to move forward with a sense of freedom.

∞ Rethinking all the tactical things: work, home life, family, and travel. It is making me rethink a lot of things. I've spent thirty-five years moving around the world, working and loving it. I miss it. I also feel a real need to invest my time, energy and heart.

  o Giving more to the friendships that are near, that often get put on the back burner for my travel and work.

  o Shifting to work with a smaller women-owned company, doing projects that are closer to home which let me develop deeper relationships in my community.

  o Making a real commitment to both social justice and compassion in this city.

  o Finding a place to volunteer that has real impact near me.

  o It also means making a bigger effort to find time to reach back to my friends around the world who have been with me on the journey.

∞ COVID-19 has changed me from a life full of people to a very solitary life. In some ways, I welcome that, it has given me a chance to "recuperate" from the stresses of the last few years of work life. With time to reboot, I can truly assess what I want to do with the rest of my life.

The outdoors have never been better!

∞ We have had to adapt to remaining at home and in our "bubble". It hasn't been all bad as it has taught me to appreciate my community more. We have discovered new walking and biking trails. We have spent more time on the golf course this past year. We have also gotten to know our neighbors more and have mastered the art of driveway gatherings.

∞ On the brighter side, our garden has never looked better and we have finally gotten around to reading those books we kept saying we would.

∞ I spend as much time outside as possible, more than pre-pandemic. I walk a great deal more than I would have without COVID-19 pushing me outside.

The effect on family and friends

The pandemic impacted our social and physical interactions with family and friends. Even with the hope of worldwide vaccinations, relationships are altered and the routine of social normalcy, as we knew it, may never be the same.

Technology has enabled us to stay connected through Zoom meet-ups or virtual happy hours, but it also robbed us of physical contact that is fundamental to our very nature of living.

The loss of family connections had profound impact.

∞ We miss our social lives terribly. I miss seeing my daughter; my eldest is having her first baby in the

126

Yukon and pandemic travel is tenuous so I can't be part of that life changing experience.

∞ I lost one of my favorite uncles in August, then my father in September – death during the pandemic is cruel.

∞ Did I get mad, sad, or both? You bet I did. Sadness was not being able to see a terminally ill friend before she passed on, then no funeral to say goodbye. My immediate family is scattered across the globe, not being able to jump on a plane to get to them in times of need was stressful.

∞ There is a loss of connection with family who live on the other side of the country and increased tension within the home.

The fear for family and friends, feeling isolated, not knowing what the future will hold.

∞ Living alone and supporting two aging parents and worrying about two young adult children in lockdown was daunting at first. But I am grateful for a great personal support network. We have all survived with our mental and physical health intact, so far. My youngest is back at home living with me, so it was nice to go into the winter with some full-time company!

∞ I miss living life without fear. I miss physical contact: a hug or a kiss from a friend.

∞ The impact of COVID-19 is mainly on our elderly parents who are increasingly isolated. One died in August, not from COVID-19, but because of it. There is a lack of care in nursing homes and hospitals where volunteers and family members are prohibited or limited.

∞ In spite of technology, the isolation is tough. I am a people person. Not seeing friends and family in person, hugging, holding hands and taking in the scents of those I love is something I realize is so important to me. I want to hug my daughter; she's in LA and we haven't seen her in over nine months now.

It wasn't just COVID-19 that changed our lives.

∞ Compounding my concern with COVID-19, the fires in California and Oregon in 2020 were frightening. The wildfires caused our skies to be filled with smoke for many weeks. My son lives in Ashland, Oregon. He had minutes to flee his house from a huge fire that burned most of a neighboring town. It took him days to get home to safety due to fires and road closures.

Social routines lost and disrupted

The inability to travel is what we missed most during the time of COVID-19. The hardship of losing the flexibility to go anywhere, be anywhere, with anyone and whomever we want, placed a burden on our happiness and well-being.

Aside from travel, social routines became lost or disrupted. Cultural events, dining out, volunteering, "gyming", and making new friends were greatly minimized or canceled entirely.

Going to the gym or recreation time needed planning. In many cases, reservations had to be made. Sports became regimented. Taking leisurely walks were needed to balance our mental and physical well-being.

Social interactions with friends and family were sorely missed.

∞ I miss the casual and organized contact with my neighbors, friends, and even acquaintances. Every chance meeting with a stranger or friend becomes a checklist of safety concerns. Am I standing far enough away? Is the mask on correctly? Do I wave, fist bump, shake hands, or hug? Is the other person a carrier, or am I?

∞ Networking can be done remotely but so much is personal, especially with new friends. I am sad to have to defer adding new friends to my network. Some connections can be made through Zoom, but it's just not the same, especially in a social, versus a business setting.

∞ Simple things like a chance encounter with a friend as I'm racing through the market, trying to shop and not get contaminated, mean so much. A recent outdoor marketplace organized by a neighbor lifted the spirits of so many people in our community.

We miss in-person community and cultural activities.

∞ I miss doing interesting things like going to concerts, theater, ballet, and art exhibits. I miss going out for dinner, going to holiday craft fairs, and going to church.

∞ I normally attend the local film festival, writer's festival, Christmas Eve carol service, library talks, art exhibition openings, cinema and open-air movies, live theatre, concerts, plus anything else that crops up. Yes, many of these events have "pivoted" to online audio-visual platforms, but it's just not the same as sitting in a dark theatre with locals, or the smell of popcorn, or the rustle of candies being unwrapped, or the air of anticipation as the lights dim.

∞ I was involved heavily in the performing arts: a large choir, a chamber choir, and community theater. Two out of three are shut down completely, the third still meets via Zoom with no near-term prospect of live rehearsals or performance.

The pandemic made even routine things harder to do.

∞ Doing things easily, like grocery shopping, visiting friends, or going out for coffee. Easy conversations with strangers.

∞ Less freedom to enjoy food shopping, which is a great pleasure for me. But, more time at home to cook and try new recipes.

∞ Our gym is limited in its offerings, like no indoor therapy pool available, which is a big deal for my physical well-being. I used to work-out two or three times a week, so this is a big loss for me both physically and mentally.

∞ Restaurants. There is nothing so glorious as ordering a special dish and having someone cook it and bring it to you while you are chatting with a friend over a glass of wine.

Before COVID-19, more than one-third of the women shared their interest to be more involved in their community. The pandemic curtailed many volunteer opportunities but also gave us others that may not have been so obvious before: volunteering for our local food bank, supporting non-profits with fundraising who are in dire need of help to sustain their operations moving forward, or supporting the most vulnerable and elderly in our community.

Janice missed her volunteer activities.
One of my favorite activities was volunteering as a municipal host for visitors at our resort. I also volunteered as a mountain guide, taking visitors on summer hikes in our mountains. Note, I wrote <u>was</u>.

Starting our COVID-19 year, all my volunteer activities were suspended. Our resort essentially shut down, and tourism became almost non-existent. Our land borders to the U.S. were closed for non-essential travel and locals didn't really need my help to find their way around.

The only travelers to our tiny resort were from other provinces, and even so, quarantine measures were the norm.

It's remains unclear as I write this whether or not these volunteering opportunities will reemerge.

While we may not be able to change the future to what we would like it to be, we can choose where we want to be. We can modify our direction when life might deal us lemons by surprise.

The impact of government

"COVID-19 affected almost all countries and more than 50-million people around the world. It has governments operating in a context of radical uncertainty, and faced with difficult trade-offs given the health, economic and social challenges it raises. By spring 2020, more than half of the world's population had experienced a lockdown with strong containment measures," according to a summary from the Organization for Economic Co-operation & Development.

"Beyond the health and human tragedy of COVID-19, it is now widely recognized that the pandemic triggered the most serious economic crisis since World War II. Many economies will not recover their 2019 output levels until 2022 at the earliest. The nature of the crisis is unprecedented: beyond the short-term repeated health and economic shocks, the long-term effects on human capital, productivity and behavior may be long-lasting."

As we looked to our governments for stability in financial support and guidance, it became apparent that until a safe vaccine could be delivered, we resigned ourselves to the new normal.

Government and national policies addressing the pandemic greatly differ throughout the world. We adjusted our routine and outlook based on the controls that were and are put upon us. We either bend to it or find another way to manage the unpredictability.

∞ Our government in New Zealand went hard and fast when the first cases of domestic transmission were detected, eradication of the virus was the goal.

Overnight we were locked at home with only supermarkets open and one person from each household going to the market. Home deliveries were prioritized for those most at risk. This lasted for four weeks with a further four weeks where small family gatherings were allowed. The border was closed, only citizens and permanent residents were allowed to enter the country. Along with lockdown being announced, the government said they would pay up to 80% of employee salaries for an initial period of twelve weeks. This saved my job.

∞ The incredible lack of leadership, support and empathy from the U.S. federal government has really been incredibly emotionally debilitating. It has been like the worst nightmare imaginable and I am concerned about the impact to our national mental health. I worry whether we will be able to heal from the virus and the emotional impact.

∞ Our government in Canada introduced an economic response plan to support Canadians facing hardship as a result of the COVID-19 outbreak. Individuals, businesses, government sectors, and First Nations benefited from financial aid programs such as wage subsidies, mortgage deferment, unemployment insurance, and others.

∞ A significant policy was the land border lockdown between Canada and the U.S. This meant no U.S. land travelers could enter Canada, unless it was deemed essential. Provinces introduced their own policies but were inconsistent across the country.

This was dependent on the severity of the cases which dictated the lockdown levels instituted.

∞ The general uncertainty and mixed messages about what's safe and not safe are unsettling. But I think the world badly needed a shake-up in terms of the environment, consumerism, commuting to work, and politics. I hope we can soon have some return to normalcy, so that plans can be made and we can pick up the long-held traditions that sustain our well-being and joy.

A final word of hope

We look forward to a world free of Covid-19. Even so, we expect the world to be different and many of the changes will be permanent. Some changes are welcome, others are challenging: working from home, vaccination requirements, seeing your doctor, shopping, wearing masks, and staying in touch via Skype, FaceTime, Zoom and more.

How we work may never revert to how it was before. Moreover, this may offer new directions that we would not have realized before the pandemic.

We put a significant amount of emphasis on well-being and health. Our individual happiness will take on a different shape. We will adapt to new changes, hopefully without resentment but with a re-energized approach.

We hope our governments can apply the learnings, knowing that nations are not invincible and that we are one global family. We hope governments take action to prevent another public global health crisis from happening again.

We hope we can be resilient and navigate future uncertainties with strength, determination and resourcefulness.

Chapter 6

The Traveler's Recipe

Travel: enrichment, meeting new people, forging new relationships or rekindling old ones.

The unique aspects of business and personal travel provide additional dimension. Business travel may be fundamental to our jobs. It expands our opportunities and builds strong foundations. Personal travel is a time to relax, rejoice in new discoveries or spend time with family and friends. This is what we yearn for when we travel.

No matter where we are in the phase of our professional lives, we travel for business or for pleasure. Some travel is very scheduled and highly planned, while other travel is more freeform or on the spur of the moment. Trips can be long or quick getaways. External demands often drive the need to travel: conferences, family, events, holidays, tragedy, and triumphs.

Travel means something different to each of us. We explore what travel means to a professional woman who may be at the top of her professional achievement in the thick-of-it, working on my-own-terms, or out-of-the-paid-work-world.

The onset of COVID-19 undeniably altered travel in ways that we never expected. In this chapter, we reflect on what business and personal travel looked like before the pandemic. We also consider what the future may hold for travel.

Then, as we entered the early days of the pandemic, our entire approach changed. For those of us in the-thick-of-it or on my-own terms, the work-from-home culture disrupted, reduced, or even eliminated business travel. We needed to figure out ways to replace the routine of business travel.

On the personal front, the pandemic put a cork in our travel plans. Virtual connections replaced the physical joy of going somewhere or being with family and friends.

Looking ahead, we know that travel will return to some degree of normalcy. Nevertheless, the rebirth of travel will take on new requirements that we will need to incorporate into our planning.

Before – when life was "normal"

Let's wind the clock back before Covid-19 when travel was an activity that was routine for many of us.

Business travel: A blessing or a burden?

For those of us whose professional career includes the need to travel for business, it can either be an exciting element of our job or a burden.

What makes business travel a positive experience?

- The opportunity to see new parts of the world and experience new cultures. "Blessed are those who see beautiful things in humble places where other people see nothing," says artist Camille Pissarro.
- Having our travel arrangements preplanned for us so we don't need to deal with all the administrivia or logistics. How nice is that!
- Allowing us the time to "be away" from work routine and office politics. What a blessing it can be, to escape the humdrum of work, boring meetings, and breakroom topics!
- It can bring diversity to our jobs and make us better appreciate the role our remote teams and colleagues have as they contribute to our success and our business.
- Depending on how far we need to travel, this time can be judiciously used to catch up on written work and to manage our priorities.

- It can enrich our careers and offer an environment where we are continually learning.

Oh, to travel for business! How lucky and blessed we are! Yes, it always starts off that way when we are young professionals. But as we move further into our careers, it can lose its wonder and excitement.

Then it happens. It starts to creep up inside of us. Business travel becomes increasingly onerous. The destinations are no longer appealing. The trips are rigorously scheduled. There is little or no time for personal exploration.

Our patience is tried: from the tedium of dealing with all the logistics, jet lag, getting to and from the airport, and queuing in lines. If we are lucky enough to be able to go to business lounges, they are overcrowded and loud.

Flying from one time zone to another starts to drain us. It impacts our productivity.

Business travel begins to rob us of our personal time. Inevitably, it creeps into our cherished weekends. We either need to leave on Sunday or return on Saturday in order to meet the demands of the job. We begin to dread the burdensome requirement to travel.

> *Janice's story of the impact of business travel.*
> As an executive for a Fortune-100 company, I had the unique opportunity to manage an international region outside of North America. At first, the rewards of business travel were exciting. I traveled to destinations I'd never been to before. I

discovered new cultures and learned new ways of doing business. I built long lasting business relationships.

But it started to take its toll. The physical stress, always having to be "on my game", and being constantly available; it was not a typical eight- or ten-hour day. Eventually, I resented the pressure it put upon me.

I felt guilty being away from my two growing sons, even more so because my spouse also had a job that required him to be away on business travel more often than not. Then all of a sudden, my older son was off to college 3,000 miles away, and it was too late for me to take back the time I lost.

For women who have a family, we often have a sense of guilt from being away too often and putting our family second to our job. We may not see that business travel offers an opportunity for personal growth because we are so focused on the responsibilities of our job.

In our interviews and survey, when we asked "What aspects will you miss <u>the least</u> from your professional life?" over forty-percent of women said they would not miss business travel at all.

This tells us that business travel generally does not give us the personal pleasures we seek or need. Business travel puts boundaries and constraints on our choices. We look at travel and the places we go through a different lens — culturally, geographically and emotionally.

Janice sees opportunities that were missed.
I remember many times during my business travel where I would yearn to take two or three hours to explore that art museum placed right at my hotel doorstep. Or take a stroll through a Japanese garden and let the exquisite natural art forms wash over me. Maybe stop by an artisan pastry shop and take a morning lesson on making French croissants. Catch a local music scene and be immersed in a new language, not caring if I understood a word!

As I look back at this aspect of my professional career, I regret not squeezing out the extra time, or adding a day up front or at the end, for "my time" — time for me to explore the newness of a city or location. There was a feeling of guilt, needing to rush back to the office or family, where I perceived I was needed more.

I convinced myself that it's okay. I'll be back. Next time I'll take that time. But I never did. Missed opportunities for personal growth, time-outs, self-reflection were left behind when I boarded the train or plane to return home.

Many of the women in the thick-of-it and on my-own-terms indicated that they will <u>not</u> miss business travel once they move out-of-the-paid-work-world. Almost 100% of women out-of-the-paid-work-world agree that they enjoy travel and are happy to not be traveling for business.

A Harvard Business Review article, titled "Just How Bad is Business Travel for Your Health?" shared some staggering data. The author found a strong correlation between the frequency of business travel and a wide range of physical and behavioral health risks. His study showed that business travel is a common threat to our health: stress, sleep interruption, unhealthy eating, too much drinking, and lack of exercise. These are common side effects of being on the road. Arguably, this likely hasn't changed in today's business environment, considering the added concern COVID-19 brings.

Personal travel: pleasures, purpose, and priorities

Regardless of whether we are in the thick-of-it, on my-own-terms or out-of-the-paid-work-world, the majority of us agree that personal travel is an activity that we most look forward to.

Spending time and strengthening our relationships with family and friends is also important for us, ranking in the top-four of ten choices. Most of us travel to build these connections to create a positive and satisfying experience. Family reunions, weddings, and other joyous occasions are planned with eagerness and happy anticipation.

What does personal or leisure travel mean to you? Travel means something different for each and every one of us. Here's what women in our survey said on what travel means and why it is so important:

- ∞ Getting in a car and driving for nine hours to see my grandchildren.
- ∞ Travel means learning, exploring interests and expanding hobbies.

∞ Travel is about relationships – strengthening the ones you have or building new ones.

∞ Do it sooner rather than later!

∞ Having fun with friends.

∞ Slowing down and enjoying life.

∞ Me time.

∞ Travel is freedom.

RANK	In the thick-of-it look forward to...	My-own-terms want to spend more time...	Out-of-paid-work-world most enjoy...
1	Travel	Strengthen relationships with family and friends	Travel
2	Improving Health and Physical Fitness	Travel	Strengthen relationships with family and friends
3	Community Involvement	Improving Health and Physical Fitness	Hobbies and interests
4	Strengthen relationships with family and friends	Personal development	Community Involvement

Maureen F's mixed bag of travel priorities.
For me, it was about getting away from day-to-day problems, and being able to put things on hold. I experienced relief being away from a difficult family situation. It was a time I could lessen my stress and think about myself. I dreaded returning home

because I knew I was returning to family problems that awaited me.

Two of my biggest ones were having kids with mental health issues, hence the dread of returning home, but also feeling guilty because I wanted to be away. What good mom feels guilty about dreading a return to children they love?

As I moved from my professional career to a time where I considered myself somewhat retired, I started to travel more with my partner, making it a part of our life journey. I'd always be there for my kids, now adults, but I reached a point in my life where I could really take the time to travel and not feel as burdened as when I was working full-time.

This new approach to travel gave me a lot of joy. I now have the good fortune to spend a couple of months and go anywhere, within my financial means, and immerse myself in new experiences, culturally and geographically.

Over half of us worry that we may not have the financial means to maintain our current lifestyle, which includes the ability to travel for our personal enjoyment. Perhaps for some of us, this means that we may never really leave the work-world so that we can have the means to travel.

Our careers may ultimately shift into paid part-time opportunities, where we can prioritize more of our personal time, yet ensure that we still have disposable income to enable us to travel.

During the pandemic – travel ... or not!

The disruption and havoc that COVID-19 delivered had monumental impact on our ability and desire to travel. Women shared that travel was the number-one thing they missed due to COVID-19 restrictions. For many, well-laid travel plans were suddenly put-on hold or canceled all together, perhaps never to be rescheduled.

2020 was also the year that business travel died, according to the Global Business Travel Association (GBTA), an association representing the global business travel industry. They estimated that there were more than 400-million business trips in the U.S. alone in 2019; that number was less than half in 2020.

Business travel became virtually non-existent, with companies rapidly deploying virtual collaboration solutions and mandating work at home policies. For some of us, eliminating business travel was a positive outcome.

Personal and leisure travel was effectively canceled as countries instituted border and quarantine controls. Some airlines stopped flying all together or went bankrupt. Right from the beginning of the pandemic, the U.S., Mexico, and Canada restricted non-essential travel across land borders. For those of us who have family or friends living in another country, our opportunity to connect requires airline travel or it doesn't happen.

Trips that we meticulously organized to "bucket list" places, or to locations where we planned a long sojourn away from our everyday routines were put aside until an unknown time.

Our personal travels to attend weddings, new births, family reunions all evaporated. Those weeks or months of anticipated travel were replaced with scrambling to undo plans, claim refunds, or reschedule with the hopes that the situation would change.

Meanwhile, we were inundated with virtual meetings, remote happy hours, and Zoom get-togethers that attempted to substitute for our physical need to be together. Travel blog posts and virtual video tours of places became the only way to "get away".

> ∞ I planned a family reunion of a lifetime. Three generations of family members heading to Norway in June 2020. It never happened. Those Norway 2020 jackets were made with love, and now collect dust on a shelf. We hope to reschedule the celebration, but we just don't know exactly when.

There are countless stories like this one. With no end in sight, we started to ponder how or when we would be able to recapture our desires for travel. With fingers crossed, we parked our travel plans in the following year or after, in hopes that we would be able to pick up where we left off.

As the pandemic raged, we realized that our only hope to regain a level of normalcy is the arrival of a vaccine. Yet that too brought unexpected complications.

The global pandemic delivered a very big detour to our lives, but we also realize that well-made plans can be offset by other things not in our control.

Janice's story of things not in our control.
In April 2019, two weeks away from a sailing trip, my husband suffered a serious accident on the ski hill. It was to be our last day of spring skiing before we embarked on our trip. We had planned this special sailing trip for over eighteen months. Needless to say, those five minutes on the ski hill changed everything.

Our travel books were put aside. Our time was now organized around numerous doctor appointments and visits to healthcare facilities. I'm very happy to say that he has recovered fully. Our trip was canceled and we were able to reschedule our entire itinerary for the following year. The following year, unbeknownst to us, the sailing trip would be canceled once again due to the pandemic.

We grappled with the inability to easily jump on a plane to be with loved ones due to COVID-19. Travel during the time of COVID-19 put constraints on our flexibility in so many ways.

Some of us have now taken to the road, literally. Why get on a plane when we can jump in our car or RV and see the sights in our own country? One woman bought a U.S. State Park pass to explore the parks with her son while another rented an RV camper and delighted in going places that they hadn't thought of before. Possibilities exist, it just means different planning.

I miss travel most of all

When asked in our second survey, "What do you miss most during the time of COVID-19?" travel leapt to the top.

∞ Before the pandemic my husband and I were super active, especially with international travel. We'd heard there are three stages of retirement: The Go-Go years, the Go-Slow years, and the No-Go years. We were taking optimal advantage of the Go-Go years, taking multiple international trips each year: Antarctica, Africa, the Arctic, and everywhere in between. I had never been happier in my life.

∞ The biggest loss is having to curb travel. Traveling has been a major part of my husband's and my life over the past 10 years.

∞ Travel is in my DNA. The lack of travel, either for business or for pleasure, really hurts. My contract implementation work dried up. Business travel provided me with company-paid trips to interesting places, along with a glimpse into diverse and interesting people.

∞ I miss family and friend gatherings, especially indoor dining at our favorite restaurants. Truly, most of all I miss travel. We canceled several trips due to COVID-19 and that has really been incredibly hard for us.

∞ I could never imagine my life being rich without learning about people, places and their culture. COVID-19 won't stop me once it's over. Perhaps I will go live somewhere else for a while. I am a kind of global nomad. It's so much part of who I am — always exploring.

After — the lure of travel

Once we resume our lives as they were before the pandemic, would business or personal travel be the same?

Chances are, it won't.

Travel will resume, and is already taking shape. Those trips to far flung places can now be rescheduled. Hefty deposits on personal trip packages that were deferred can now be recouped and planned. Weddings, family reunions, the sailing trip of a lifetime, or yearly getaways can now be realized.

But things have changed. Our planning is different. We put different priorities on our travel quotient. We may even think of destinations and modes of transportation in different ways.

As we sit back, overloaded on news of COVID-19, the variants, and the vaccine rollout, we feel a glimmer of hope in the new normal.

The post-pandemic normal will take on a new reality of its own. We'll take stock of what's really important to us. Our happiness, well-being and healthcare will be reassessed and amplified.

The traveler's recipe

Thinking about re-entering the world of travel is somewhat like creating a recipe for a meal. Our recipe will differ for business and personal travel.

Business travel will re-emerge. For those of us who travel for business, our choices may be limited. We may not have much control on how, when or where we need to be, especially if we are required to do our jobs effectively. Some of the perks we enjoyed in the past may no longer be available, such as business lounges, preferred hotels or level of travel.

On the other hand, personal travel offers flexibility with our choices. Even so, personal travel, will face new controls such as vaccination documents or mandated health insurance. Cancelations and other itinerary changes may not be as flexible, or choices may be limited depending on new regulations as a result of COVID-19. Costs will likely be much higher – those special deals may not be so special anymore and the competition for preferred rates will be high.

Traveling for business or pleasure can yield either a great experience or a dismal venture. Make the most of it by having a plan and being prepared. Just like creating that awesome gourmet meal, select your secret ingredients and form them into your travel feast.

Preparation can involve numerous steps – shopping for the best deal, making sure passport and visas are up-to-date, checking health advisories, getting necessary vaccinations and prescriptions, and preparing to enjoy yourself. Get the information necessary to ensure your trip will have the best outcome.

We now have a new checklist.

- ✓ Is the world still as accessible as it was pre COVID-19? Are some places off-limits?
- ✓ Do we need proof of vaccination, such as a digital passport or card?
- ✓ Is a negative COVID-19 test required even if I am vaccinated?
- ✓ Will I need to quarantine? How long? Where?
- ✓ Our health concerns have expanded. Travel insurance is now a necessity.
- ✓ Pack your mask, you may still need it.
- ✓ Prepare for high demand.

We will be faced with the fact that the cost of traveling will be higher. Some carriers and hoteliers have even gone out of business. Some routes no longer exist and may never be reinstated. Flights are oversold. Rental cars are not as readily available and one-way rentals are difficult to find. Our choices may change from cruises to outdoor adventures, from flying to driving.

Business travel menu – rigid or flexible?

One can argue that when traveling for business, constraints are already put upon us; our desires or personal options take a back seat. Business travel typically "dictates" the plan we are expected to follow. There is usually very little wiggle room to incorporate personal choices unless they don't directly impact business routine.

If managed a bit differently, business travel can create a positive balance between the professional requirements of your job and your personal needs.

Think of this as bleisure: Business + leisure travel = bleisure travel.

WFH blurred the lines between work and home. So, let's blur the distinction between business and personal travel.

With appealing destinations, pre-pandemic professionals around the globe were increasingly adding weekends, or even weeks, to business trips. Whether solo, with a partner, or as a family, work trips can be extended.

The concept of bleisure is about making the most of your business trips. It offers improved morale, increased enjoyment, and needed relaxation. Include a quick holiday weekend as an add-on to your business travel.

Bleisure travel isn't new and we didn't create the concept. It's been growing since the term first appeared in 2009, coined by Future Laboratory. It gained momentum, as Expedia Group Media Solutions found in a 2018 study that showed bleisure travelers turned 60% of their business trips into vacations.

Remote office working, WFH, and virtual schooling became pandemic norms, not out of desire but from necessity. Even so, this creates opportunities for bleisure travelers, especially if you can drive to one place or another. Working remotely doesn't necessarily mean from *your* home. You could be at another desirable destination. Why not work from a resort – WFR: working-from-resort. Most hotels now cater to longer stays with families in mind, and some even have programs for tutoring and after-school electives.

Business or bleisure travel will continue to evolve post-COVID-19. The WFH model will stay but not likely 100% in its current form. It will morph into a blend of working remotely and at a company location. Business travel will slowly creep back into the requirements of the job. Customer facing activities will once again become face-to-face, not just virtual.

We re-enter the world of business travel cautiously. Health concerns and travel restrictions are present, be it back of mind or prime concern. We navigate new rules and policies.

Bleisure practices can take on a different form. Not just tacking on a weekend here or there. Longer stays at a resort or hotel become part of our culture because we have learned that we can do our work effectively from almost anywhere. We have the opportunity to reinvent business travel to better fit our personal desires.

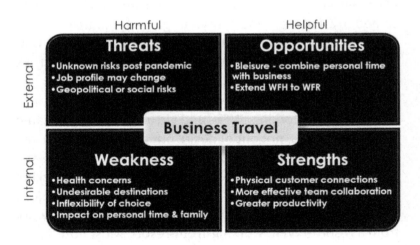

	Harmful	Helpful
External	**Threats** • Unknown risks post pandemic • Job profile may change • Geopolitical or social risks	**Opportunities** • Bleisure - combine personal time with business • Extend WFH to WFR
	Business Travel	
Internal	**Weakness** • Health concerns • Undesirable destinations • Inflexibility of choice • Impact on personal time & family	**Strengths** • Physical customer connections • More effective team collaboration • Greater productivity

When building your business travel recipe, consider the external and internal factors alongside of those which are helpful or harmful. Do the helpful factors outweigh the personal risks? Carefully weigh the things out of your control and what impact they may play in your decision. With time, these may shift from one direction to the other.

Build your personal travel checklist

Define yourself.

- ✓ Do you operate on rigid structure or loose format, preferring the comfort of knowing all the details in advance or "seeing how it flows?"
- ✓ Your approach to pleasure travel may have changed since the onset of the pandemic. You may find that you no longer want to risk travel to a foreign country that might still be struggling with the effects of the pandemic.

Define your passions.

- ✓ Think about the things that bring you pleasure, such as art and culture or exploring the great outdoors. You may seek calm soothing relaxation or thrilling adventure that pushes you to new limits.
- ✓ Perhaps you like to travel alone. Maybe you enjoy traveling with groups of like-minded people who share the same interests, or with your partner or spouse. Sun and sand may be your desired destination, or mountains and trees give you the most pleasure.

✓ Whatever you prefer, there are unchartered places as well as tried-and-true recommendations from Lonely Planet and Fodor. You can plan for surprises or just be surprised. Comfort and routine can be combined with the rugged and eccentric. Maybe a unique combination is in order.

My Personal Travel Profile

Define your motivation.

✓ It may be expansive or keenly focused on specific events such as spending time with family and friends, relaxing and rejuvenating, or getting away from normal everyday life.

✓ The type of travel is up to you: bucket list, summer vacation, weekend getaway, celebration, solo travel, international, domestic travel. Balance your motivation with your financial ability.

✓ Travel can also be wrapped around the need to provide care for a partner or aging parents. Travel means getting to the place or location where care is required. Aging parents or relatives may not live in the same city or even country. Travel can be a requirement, and not necessarily the form of enjoyment hoped for.

Some women in our survey regretted not taking more time for leisure travel sooner. Unforeseen events made pleasure travel less viable: a partner's major health decline, an accident, aging in-laws or parents, or the pandemic.

Janice's personal push and pull of travel.
I was in the height of my career, living in a country that was on the other side of the world. It would take me two full days and six time zones to travel to my parents' home in eastern Canada.

Visiting my parents became an activity I would fit into my personal vacation time, and that worked well for a number of years. I even got smarter and would fly my mom out to visit us, an opportunity she always looked forward to.

I'm so grateful to have been able to share this travel with her. But then she got ill. She couldn't travel those long distances anymore. Trips to see her and my dad had to be at their home, on their terms, so this became part of my planning.

Then the inevitable happened. My dad suddenly died. I couldn't get home in time. I told myself I should have taken the time to visit more often. I should have put aside those other travel experiences. These were the guilty thoughts I had; I struggled with self-doubt.

I made a pact with myself that I'd visit mom even more often. It became more important as her own health started to decline, and my sisters became the primary caregivers. I'd carve out two weeks at a time to spend with her, giving my sisters the break they deserved from their caregiving duties. I was fortunate to have a job that allowed me to work remotely and a company whose business culture accepted this.

Needless to say, my idea of travel took on a whole different purpose: the need to be with my mom, the importance of supporting of my sisters, and reconnecting with my extended family and friends who I'd left behind thirty-plus years earlier.

Packing the suitcase

You gotta go where you wanna go
Do what you wanna do
With whoever you wanna do it with
The Mamas and Papas, 1966

Imagine being able to have the means to go wherever you'd like. Imagine having the time and money to immerse yourself in new experiences, culturally and geographically. It is possible. The means, the time and money are there. You may need to scale your plans to match your means.

Available time may depend on where you are in your relationship to work. If you are in the thick-of-it, time may be at a premium. Working on my-own-terms may provide flexibility to manage your time to your liking. For women out-of-the-paid-work-world, time might be plentiful depending on other constraints such as physical health or lifestyle changes.

Travel requires money. Cost is always a consideration, no matter what your financial means or where you are in relation to the work-world. The glorious thing is that travel options abound from budget travel to five-star gold-plated, and everything in between. Even with generous financial resources, choosing a budget-friendly travel deal may offer just what you are looking for.

As one woman learned, planning is so important. "You might think you've found the ideal place or country because you put a significant amount of effort in your research, only to find out after two months of being there, you never felt welcomed by the locals." Things may also be very different living in a post-pandemic world.

If your travel location is a place where you'll "live" or work for a longer period of time, pick the spot carefully. Know what you want to do. Consider all the reasons why you want to travel there. Set your expectations so you won't be disappointed. Maybe it's not important to meet new people and create new memories. That's OK. If you will be working while you are there, make sure reliable business resources are available to you if you are WFH (working from home) or WFR (working from resort).

As the pandemic settles down, our desires for travel will either be amplified or diminished. Either way, we still get to make those choices. The choices may not be as easy as before, but we'll figure it out.

Chapter 7

A Curiosity: Leaving the Paid Work-World

In our age of freedom, some women choose to leave the paid work-world behind. Why would they do this? We want to understand this option taken by a quarter of the women in our survey. Janet has also chosen this option, or perhaps more accurately, she evolved into it.

In order to peek behind the scenes, we asked women out-of-the-paid-work-world two questions:

- *The Magic Question:* What do you wish you knew in advance?
- *The Surprise:* For you, what was the biggest surprise?

The answers to these two questions give us a peek inside the option of leaving the paid work-world behind. It is a sort of crystal ball looking into the mysteries of a future without paid work.

Our lives are not preordained, our destiny is not being decided for us. You don't have to leave the paid work-world if you don't want to. Destiny is what you are meant to do. You have a choice in that. Fate is what happens when you don't take responsibility; it is also a choice—the choice not to make an active or conscious decision.

"Destiny is not always preordained. Life is about making choices. Our lives are the sum of all the choices we make, the bridges we cross, and the ones we burn. Our souls cast long shadows over many people, even after we are gone. Fate, luck, and providence are the consequence of our freedom of choice, not the determinants. When justice is served by following our principles, making good decisions brings us inner peace." Judith Land says it eloquently and directly in her book *Adoption Detective: Memoir of an Adopted Child*.

In business we learn from mentors, role models, and pace setters. In our life choices we can do the same. That is why we asked women out-of-the-paid-work-world about their experiences – the good, the bad, and the surprises.

We laugh quietly to ourselves, at ourselves, and at each other for not always looking ahead to what our options are or were. How often we have heard that people spend more time planning their vacations than:

- Their finances, according to CBC, Money, and CNBC.
- Their careers, declared Zig Ziglar.
- Their life, as Michael Hyatt tells us.

162

We are all guilty of that, at least a little bit. We don't have to be. Not now. Not in our age of freedom. Listen to what women out-of-the-paid-work-world have to say and learn from their collective experience.

This chapter is not one voice, one opinion, or one experience. This is the voice of experience from all of those women in our survey who are out-of-the-paid-work-world.

Relationship to Work-World

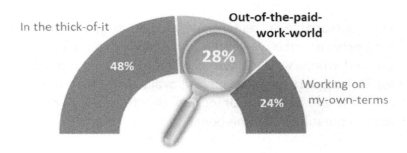

Take it all in. You may agree with some insights, disagree with others, and ponder other ones in confusion. You are unique, one of a kind. The unique you will know what to do with the information. You will incorporate some of the information into your life and some you will leave behind on the shelf to collect dust. It's the beauty and power of being you in the age of freedom!

The magic question

Both professionally and personally, all of us seek to unlock the mysteries of the future.

In business, investors look for the most promising ventures. Financial managers seek accurate business projections. Production managers pursue critical deadlines. Healthcare professionals, strive for healthy outcomes. Educators look to promote learning and mastering new concepts.

On a personal level, as humans we seek to make the best life decisions: who we keep close, what we spend our time on, and where we live. We look for friendship and search for lifelong partners. We explore available options to make the best life choices. Unlocking the future has been a human pursuit since time began.

For women in the thick-of-it or working on my-own-terms, a question might be, "Would I want to leave the paid work-world behind at some point in my life?" It's not a magic question. It's just an option.

To help ponder this option, we asked women out-of-the-paid-work-world, "What do you wish you knew in advance?" This is a magic question, because it has the value of knowledge gained through experience. The experience of making the choice to cross a bridge, then turning back to look at the crossing, and reflect on what could have been done differently or better.

The responses to this magic question range from disappointment to delight and contain many noteworthy suggestions and recommendations. We view it as a best practice approach evidenced by our research and real-life field lessons learned by the women in our survey.

We discovered that there is no easy button, "one BIG thing", or single magic answer. Successfully moving out-of-the-paid-work-world is a combination of things: structure, reinvention, preparation, timing, and partnership.

Magic answer: structure

There is an impact to having no defined schedule or time demands. One fifth of the women commented on how daily demands change.

Beware: What you used to do in your spare time now takes all day.

- ∞ I miss the structure.
- ∞ How much longer it takes to do things.
- ∞ I gave myself permission to not accomplish twenty goals per day.
- ∞ I definitely got a lot more done while I was working.
- ∞ How many day-to-day things there are to do and how wonderfully unrushed the days are.
- ∞ It's okay not to rush everything and not feel guilty about it.

Trust yourself.

- ∞ Be gentle and practice kindness with yourself and others.

∞ If you are self-directed, motivated and productive in your working years, you will be the same as you choose your own path.

∞ The essence of you does not change.

Enjoy the flexibility of choosing how to spend your time. A "freedom of choice" echoes again and again.

∞ Not being controlled by the clock.

∞ How much I like setting my own agenda and schedule.

∞ How much I enjoy the freedom of making my own schedule and setting my needs as a priority.

∞ The pleasure of a quiet day is good for my soul and not boring as I had feared.

Be confident in your ability to find interesting and fulfilling activities. "No need to ever worry about being bored," is repeated loud and often.

∞ I finally have time for volunteer activities that really interest me.

∞ I'm surprised at how busy I am.

∞ I enjoy the activities and community organizations I engage with.

∞ There are tons of things to do to stay busy, involved, and happy.

∞ I eventually had to say no to some things I got involved in, because I left no time for myself.

Establish a routine and keep a to-do list (Janet keeps a bullet journal).

∞ I wish I knew how great it could be to set my own agenda and have the time to pursue the projects and interests that I care about.

∞ I get to do more things, without the job constraints.

∞ Set a routine early on. It can be a daily, weekly, or monthly routine.

∞ Find something structured to do; I still want a schedule with some commitments and some empty time.

Janet's secret love affair.
Have you had a secret love affair in your life? I have. As I reflect on this insight of routine and schedules, I guess it is time to tell you about my secret love affair with my calendar.

We have been together a long time. I don't know how long it has been, but it seems like forever. We are inseparable, always together. Yet, separate and distinct.

We have both changed a lot over the years. I laugh when I think about the transformations. Bigger, smaller, wider, taller. Sometimes busy, bossy, and demanding, while other times idle and disengaged. From pen-and-paper to PalmPilot to Outlook to smartphone. Ha!

We have been through a lot together. The good times, when life was fast-paced and everything clicked. So many options and so many things going on, that sometimes it seemed impossible to navigate through them all, but we did it somehow. Together.

There were also bad times. Which I prefer to think of as tough times or difficult times rather than bad. Bad just sounds so …. bad. Some days it was just going through the motions. Other days were a blur. But we got through it together.

There was a time when I thought I didn't need you anymore. I set you aside. As a result, important things were missed, like the dinner engagement with Mike and Virginia, who will never forgive me, especially Mike. Well, that won't happen again.

We go everywhere together. We still do. We are inseparable. If we are not doing it together, we are not doing it. During our work years you always took the lead and I was your side-kick, now in my age of freedom it's more often the other way around.

We constantly check in with one another. Well, you are better than I am; I easily get sucked into the moment and lose track. If we weren't looking at each other, we were wondering what the other one was up to. I am lost without you. When we are separated, it's confusing and disorienting; even aggravating and upsetting. Something is missing, the little things seem like a mystery.

The funny thing about our relationship is that it is filled with constant questions. What are you up to?

What's next? Where are we going? What's happening this weekend? Can we sleep in? Together, we know the answers. Or you know the answers and it's up to me to take action.

We rely on each other. I can't imagine life without you. YOU, my calendar. My schedule. My diary. My day-planner. No matter what the name, I can't live without you. Today you are on my smartphone and with me almost every minute of the day. If I leave you at home, I turn the car around and go back to get you. We are, forever, together in time.

Magic answer: reinvent yourself

There is an impact to being out-of-the-paid-work-world, whether you are stepping out of the thick-of-it or rewriting the conditions of working on my-own-terms. A quarter of the women tell us to use our creativity and reinvent ourselves.

An *invention* is a unique or novel device, method, composition, or process that can be an improvement upon something existing or creating something new. Some of the most important inventions of mankind are the printing press, light bulb, airplane, personal computer, vaccines, automobile, clock, and telephone.

A *reinvention* is the action or process through which something is changed so much that it appears to be entirely new. You are the most important reinvention of you!

Janet talks of reinvention.
I have had to reinvent myself many times.

My first job out of college was in the field of education (college admissions), shifting into the high-tech world I had to reinvent myself into a high-tech salesperson. Many of the skills were transferable but needed expansion, new knowledge, and different talents.

The move from individual contributor to manager was my next significant reinvention. The new management world was all about my team, not just about setting my own goals and priorities. The focus was on common and aligned goals. Collaboration. Inclusiveness. Teamwork. Partnership. I had to reinvent myself from doing to delegating and to knowing the whole business, not just my little piece of the work world.

My next reinvention was the move from manager to executive. Then another reinvention as I moved from a well-established company to a start-up.

The move to working on my-own-terms was especially dramatic. But you already heard that story in *Chapter 3: Let Your Reach Exceed Your Grasp*.

Truth is, I never used the word reinvention through any of those career changes. It was just progress, growth or an alternation. I probably used the terms turning point or focal point more often as I changed my behavior, attitude, or approach. But it's the same thing.

Reinvention experienced by women out-of-the-paid-work-world is not something strange and different. You will likely find parallels in your own personal or professional life. Here are the voices of women reflecting on their journey and their transition.

Love those working years and love the not working years. "How great life is," echoes loud and clear from those out-of-the-paid-work-world.

∞ After thirty years I was ready to sell my company, which I loved; and now I love my new life.

∞ I enjoy not having to go to work every day and put up with some of the idiocy of modern business.

∞ I definitely don't miss the stress, the worry, or the anxiety!

∞ Loved it when I was working and love it now that I am not!

∞ It never occurred to me that I would **not** miss working.

∞ I am very fulfilled.

Reinvent yourself.

∞ Work provides a simple, easy identity. I kinda lost my identity and had to reinvent myself.

∞ I am no longer an Assistant Dean or a CEO; so, who am I now?

∞ I was worried about not being taken seriously.

∞ The first six-months were a tough transition for me, feeling that I am not contributing, then this new world opened up and revealed itself to me.

∞ I am not my career or my job title. I am happy and productive.

You will miss the people from your work life.

∞ I miss the involvement with my colleagues.

∞ I miss working with students and their families.

∞ I was surprised that people I worked with did not invite me to participate in Christmas parties and special events.

∞ I miss the interactions with my peers.

∞ I was surprised at how fast I became "out of the loop".

People you want to spend time with may not be available.

∞ My friends are still in the thick-of-it.

∞ My children and grandchildren lead such busy lives.

∞ I am available but others are not.

∞ My closest friends and family live too far away to visit or do things with, except for special occasions.

∞ Maintaining friendships with colleagues that are still working is challenging.

Relationships that matter will not be lost.

∞ I retain relationships with colleagues I enjoy.

∞ You will stay in touch with the people who matter.

∞ The company is not your family.

Make new friends.

- ∞ I didn't foresee how lonely it could be.
- ∞ Having few people around most of the day — the isolation.
- ∞ It can be hard to make new deep friendships; it takes time.
- ∞ My activities and interests helped me develop new personal relationships and forge new friendships.
- ∞ My hobbies keep me engaged with more people.

Magic answer: preparation

As professional women, we wouldn't walk into a business situation unprepared. Why should life be any different? Don't move out-of-the-paid-work-world unprepared.

Nearly half of the women who are out-of-the-paid-work-world told us of the importance of preparation. It's not like stepping off an airplane onto the environmentally controlled jet-bridge and into a sparkling airport terminal filled with convenient shops and restaurants. Leaving the work-world is more like stepping into an *Indiana Jones* movie; it's exciting and unpredictable, with its own rewards.

Prepare: personally, financially, and for the unexpected.

Personal preparation

Have an exit strategy and reinvention plan.

- ∞ I was well prepared by reading up on what's involved when making a full departure from the work-world.
- ∞ I feel like I had it wired.

Look ahead and anticipate your needs.

- ∞ Develop interests, hobbies, and activities outside of work.
- ∞ I would like to have had better ways to organize my lifestyle, be healthier, and more in tune with my community.
- ∞ I wish I had paid more attention to retirement information earlier in my career.
- ∞ I wish I knew how to mentally prepare for leaving the work-world.

Learn from the experience of others.

- ∞ Have one or more mentors who have made this transition.
- ∞ It was important for me to find the right mentors / managers to help guide my continued improvement.
- ∞ It was helpful to have friends who had gone before me, that made it seem like much less of a "risk".
- ∞ It was difficult to step down from a highly paid, upwardly mobile VP level job in a $1.5 billion corporation to pursue other ambitions, starting at ground zero.

Pursue a work-life balance.

- ∞ A good work-home balance makes for a smoother transition.
- ∞ Work relationships and accomplishments were short lived; they disappeared as soon as I left my career ... I would have strived for a better work-life balance.

Assess your skills.

- ∞ When I left my career job it took me over a year to figure out where I could apply my skills.
- ∞ I could be happier doing other things, change is good. I'll figure it out. It's not the end of the world.
- ∞ It took me a while to figure out what other opportunities my skills would transfer to.

Fiscal preparation

I wish I knew...

- ∞ That I would be safe and financially comfortable.
- ∞ That retirement is great and affordable.
- ∞ That the loss of a steady paycheck could be so scary.
- ∞ How expensive it can be.
- ∞ That I needed to switch my thinking about finances from earning a salary to being on a fixed income.

Time your benefits to your best advantage.

- ∞ I wish I had waited to take U.S. Social Security until I was seventy.

∞ As a nurse I was able to work "per diet" or part-time for the last five years of my career; however, this choice forfeited a lot of my monthly pension.

∞ I was happy to learn that I could take spousal social security benefits (U.S.) and wait until age 70 to maximize my own benefits.

Understand health insurance options. "The high cost of medical care," echoed through the responses.

∞ The expense of healthcare.

∞ My health insurance dramatically changed for the worse and prescription drug costs soared at the same time.

∞ Rising medical costs.

∞ I assumed that U.S. Medicare would be the same as company health insurance, but it's not.

Organize and be aware of living expenses.

∞ Yikes, I needed to plan money for 40 years!

∞ Little things like groceries and eating out, become big things and a major cost consideration.

∞ I had to learn to manage my finances more effectively and budget.

∞ U.S. Social Security (or other government programs, like Canadian Social Insurance) doesn't cover as much as you might think.

∞ I had to change my financial management thinking and approach from "income flow" to "cash flow".

Invest.

- ∞ I didn't anticipate the impact of a recession and how it took away the high interest coming in.
- ∞ I should have increased my U.S. IRA and 401K investments (similar to the Canadian RRSP and national retirement plans in other countries).
- ∞ I would have been less generous and saved more.
- ∞ I wish I spent more time understanding financial investments or getting a financial advisor.

Unpredictable preparation

Family health changes can have a huge impact.

- ∞ How little time we had with my in-laws before they could no longer travel.
- ∞ I was not prepared for the financial, emotional, and time demands that would be placed on me in order to care for my aging parents.
- ∞ As my elderly parents' health began to fail, it was a gift to be able to step out of the work-world with ample time and energy to fully support and care for them.
- ∞ My husband developed health problems that limit our ability to do things we used to enjoy together.
- ∞ Don't postpone your dreams: my husband and I had delayed major travel plans for when we both retired, then he had a major health decline that year.

Your own health changes can have a huge impact.

> ∞ There are so many things I thought I would do, but I am no longer capable of doing because of my health issues; it's disappointing.

Relationships can change.

> ∞ "My husband/partner left me." Sadly, three women told us this.

You may lose someone you care about.

> ∞ The difficulty of losing a member of my age cohort.
>
> ∞ Losing my spouse to death.
>
> ∞ My husband died leaving me overwhelmed with depression; it is so hard without him but I'm happy that I had those last two-years with him.
>
> ∞ My mother took sick and passed away shortly after I stepped out of the work-world; I would have made the transition earlier to have more time with her.

Magic answer: timing

Many women ask, "What is the right time to step out-of-the-paid-work-world?" Our answer is: "That's up to you." Your right time is your right time. Then again, maybe the right answer for you is never.

Maybe sooner: "I would have made the transition sooner if I knew how great it would be," is heard echoing again and again.

∞ If I had known how great my life would be, I may have left the work-world sooner … yes, may have, even though I loved my working years.

∞ Just love my time and my free time; I worked hard for it.

∞ I have become much kinder, compassionate, and fulfilled.

∞ I could have left the work-world earlier.

Maybe later: Hmmm. Not one woman out-of-the-paid-work-world said they should have waited before making the transition which, for us, confirms that your right time is your right time. We have so many choices in our age of freedom.

Maybe never: Yes, it is your choice to not leave the paid work-world. Some women in the thick-of-it and on my-own-terms voiced the opinion that they didn't want or expect to leave the paid work-world. It's their choice in their age of freedom.

Whose decision is this?

If you are going out-of-the-paid-work-world on your own, you have a few additional things to consider. You may be going into this solo, but you are not alone.

According to Forbes, roughly one-third of all 45- to 63-year-olds are single. Most have never married or are separated due to divorce, death, or choice. The same considerations for preparation, the need to reinvent yourself, and the need for structure remain important. But several women shared the unique considerations they faced.

∞ Make new friends and strengthen the relationships with old friends; identify your most trusted friends, they are your family.

∞ Without a spouse or children, it's easy to become isolated; immerse yourself in activities that you enjoy that include other people.

∞ Figure out who your "chosen family" is, the mutual support is rewarding.

If you share your life with someone else, it needs to be a mutual decision.

∞ I had to wait for my partner to leave the work-world.

∞ I remained in the thick-of-it for seven years more than my husband and hadn't realized how much it affected him.

∞ I didn't realize how my husband really felt about me leaving the work-world so much earlier than he.

∞ Spending so much more time with my spouse took some getting used to.

Janet's transition out-of-the-paid-work-world.
My husband and I both worked on our-own-terms for several years before fully stepping out-of-the-paid-work-world; transitioning together made it comfortable for both of us.

Working on our-own-terms had us both traveling internationally. My husband spent months in Africa working both in and on a new business venture. I was facilitating workshops around the world for two different clients. I even had the pleasure of meeting my husband in Africa for a week, in the midst of a crazy five-week business trip that took me to five continents!

With both of us working on our-own-terms, we eased into being together full-time. We eased into preparation together, as we faced questions about what was ahead. We eased into reinventing ourselves, both individually and as a couple. It does take some effort; we were not the same dual-career couple that we were before. We eased into restructuring our time and our lives.

We transitioned together. We talked about various aspects of our life together as the transition occurred, some conversations were via Skype and others in-person over a glass of wine. We have always been blessed with a great relationship and by making this transition together that relationship is even stronger.

Okay, I don't want to sound too pie-in-the-sky or falsely optimistic. Like taking a Jeep or a mountain bike on the back roads, it was bumpy and there were (and still are) a few potholes that can swallow us up. There are the annoying little habits. There are the disagreements. He wants to do everything together. Really? He even wants to go grocery shopping with me ... really? I've got this handled. Lots of little things seem to require negotiation.

We are still transitioning three years into it. COVID-19 had us working on it even more with full-immersion marriage. Maybe transitioning is a life's work. We are fortunate to both want a lifelong relationship.

As Mom Gregory says, "A relationship is 50-50, half-and-half. The math works out to 60-40 and 40-60, so roll with it."

We are rolling with it.

The answers to the magic question contain action-oriented advice from those that chose to move out-of-the-paid-work-world.

Prepare personally, financially, and for the unpredictable. Be confident in yourself. Preparation doesn't need to be perfect, just good enough so that you can feel confident to take action if and when you choose.

The surprise

Life is full of surprises.

It turns out there is even science to explain surprises, if you ask a psychologist or neuroscientist. There is even a mathematical formula that explains surprise, which was a surprise to us. The Bayesian Theory is that surprise can only exist in an uncertain environment. Surprise must depend upon prior expectations or experience. The Bayesian theorems are in the image below.

182

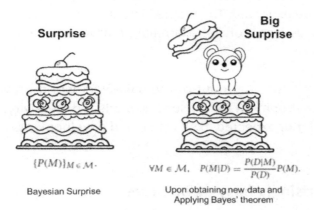

Surprise

Big Surprise

$\{P(M)\}_{M \in \mathcal{M}}.$

$\forall M \in \mathcal{M}, \quad P(M|D) = \dfrac{P(D|M)}{P(D)} P(M).$

Bayesian Surprise

Upon obtaining new data and Applying Bayes' theorem

In our professional life, we typically don't like surprises. At work, most surprises are bad news, unfavorable variations from expectations like losing a major customer, a patient's dramatic turn for the worse, a production line failure, or a student's significant decline in performance. We don't mind the infrequent good surprises of unexpected recognition, a big win, or a raise in pay.

Life is much the same. We don't like the bad surprises or receiving bad news. But good surprises can be lots of fun, like a surprise party or the unexpected appearance of someone you haven't seen in ages.

We asked women out-of-the-paid-work-world, "For you, what was the biggest surprise?"

Their answers are introspective, personal, and confident. It was about tackling something unfamiliar, gaining knowledge, succeeding, and learning in the process. It contains a certain power and unexpected reward.

183

Their surprises were more thoughtful and contemplative than we expected. The women in our survey paused to look inside as a sort of self-examination aroused by our simple question.

It seems that time out-of-the-paid-work-world provides a rich environment for personal growth and creativity. It is a time for unexpected exploration and development.

Surprisingly busy – a*nd more*

Many women out-of-the-paid-work-world say they are surprised at "how busy I am." Because this response came from more than one-third of the women, it means that their surprise is the result of encountering something completely unexpected – being busy. We suspect that their expectation was a life of idleness, emptiness, or being bored.

Where does this expectation of inertia, idleness, or boredom come from? Did it come from role models – mother, father or maybe others that they knew well? Was it their own experience – the intensity of working versus the leisure of vacation?   Could it stem from a silent fear or phobia – belief that not working is something dangerous, likely to cause harm or pain or boredom?

Where the expectation of idleness comes from is not apparent from our research, but it is likely to be some combination of personal experience, the experience of a role model, or dread. Wherever it comes from, it's real for many women.

More questions arose for us. Was this busy-ness good or bad? So, what kind of busy is it? Is it the industrious-diligent-devoted kind of busy? Or is it the caged-hamster-on-a-running-wheel kind of busy? As we spent more time with the responses, something fascinating and more profound emerged.

A few women made the simple unadorned statement, "How busy I am," with no additional comment. There was an occasional pondering, "How did I have time to work?" Yet, we know nothing more about their high level of activity.

The vast majority are surprisingly busy **and more**. They are fulfilled in a meaningful way. What keeps them busy is their expanded interests and cultivation of self. So, we will leave the few with no additional comment to stand on their own "busy-ness". As you read on, we have combined the **and more** with the other responses.

Surprised how the world expanded

Dramatic new insights emerged from the women in our survey: possibilities are there if you are open to them.

When one door closes, another door opens,
but we often look so long and so regretfully
upon the closed door,
that we do not see
the ones which have opened for us.

Versions of this quote have been attributed to both Alexander Graham Bell and Helen Keller. There is tremendous wisdom in this quote. Whether you are a great inventor or the first deaf-blind person to receive a bachelor's degree or if you are reinventing yourself out-of-the-paid-work-world. Read the quote one more time for its powerful perception.

Discover brave new directions.

∞ I immediately became interested in things using the right side of my brain … art, photography, music. Stepping away from my analytical work-side opened me up to find surprising new talents.

∞ How varied my interests are and how much I am learning now.

∞ I suppose that I unknowingly utilized my creative side in business, but I never believed I was creative until I stepped out of the busy work-world.

∞ Time to explore and satisfy my curiosities.

Encounter a new world.

∞ The chance to appreciate a successful career, then move on to new things.

∞ So many pleasant surprises: personal friends, time to engage in social and cultural activities, time to enjoy nature's beauty.

∞ How much I enjoy new encounters.

∞ I travel a lot!

∞ My home is the world; how comfortable it is to travel for five or six months during the year.

Embrace a "second career".

- ∞ I co-authored a book that took three years to write.
- ∞ I fundamentally have a second career now, one that pays much less but something that I love to do; I'll need to retire again someday!
- ∞ I was very surprised at how successful I would be in my second career.
- ∞ That at the age of eighty, I would be publishing my seventh book.
- ∞ How busy I am with three board memberships, my "career" as a symphonic musician, traveling for fun, and traveling to see my kids in college.

Janet's reinvention.
Two things have evolved into second careers and my new identity. One is getting my pilot's license and learning to fly. It opened my world to the great joy of flight and very active volunteer work at aviation events around the county. The other is writing, along with two other women who shared this as their second careers above.

The door to writing opened slowly while I was working on my-own-terms. It started with work-related articles and blogs. It evolved into writing monthly articles for our small local newspaper.

The work-related articles and blogs resulted in my first publication, a business book, *Built for Global.*

The monthly articles resulted in my second publication, as ghostwriter of an autobiography,

Hanna's Story. Hanna is one of my amazing neighbors. She escaped from Nazi Germany during the bombing of Dresden, married a U.S. soldier, and homesteaded a ranch in Wyoming. I was enthralled with her story and knew it needed to be captured.

The monthly articles also led to motivating others in our community to write their memoirs or family stories. As a result, I co-facilitate writer workshops at our local library for other aspiring and experienced writers looking to build their craft.

Writing has evolved into a great joy for me. It is now a "second career" of sorts. The more I write, the more I learn about writing and expand my interest in a wide variety of topics. I have five writing projects on my white board at the moment. Not all of these writing projects will end up as books, as there are so many other outlets. I am enjoying learning, developing, and sharing my love for writing.

Surprisingly fulfilled

Feelings of contentment, satisfaction, and happiness are woven into the vast majority of responses to our question of surprise. When not distracted by the demands of the work-world there is time for fulfillment beyond business objectives and performance measures. There is time to create positive experiences that are important, feel good, and fulfill a sense of purpose.

How easy it is to find a focus that is completely engaging.

- ∞ How effortless and easy it is to fill my day with meaningful activities.
- ∞ I feel energized most days, and I finally have time for volunteer activities that really interest me.
- ∞ How much I enjoy doing community work.
- ∞ I fill my day with lots of little activities – dog walking, playing the piano, reading, and staying organized.
- ∞ I am busy, still very active, and continue to find fulfilling activities after ten years.
- ∞ How engaged I still feel.
- ∞ The satisfaction I get from volunteer work.
- ∞ My life is full with family, travel, and more. I don't have time for work.

Wondering how everything got done while working.

- ∞ I don't know how I ever worked full-time and managed to be a caring, thoughtful mother and wife, in addition to taking time for myself.
- ∞ I do more things without the constraints of a job.
- ∞ I don't miss work at all, there are many other wonderful things to do when work doesn't occupy so much of my time and energy.
- ∞ I enjoy setting my own schedule.
- ∞ How did I ever get everything done when working and traveling for business?
- ∞ Bored? Sometimes yes, maybe. Mostly no, never. When I find myself being bored it's because I have lots of things to do but not necessarily things I enjoy.

In the absence of clearly defined goals
we become strangely loyal
to performing daily acts of trivia.
Robert Heinlien, American science-fiction author

How important it is to have a purpose.

∞ I fill my time so easily … no chance of being bored.

∞ How disorganized I can get without goals and objectives.

∞ My day needs a game plan after being a hostage of my work schedule and spending long days at work.

∞ Structure is key for me; I plan my week out.

∞ I love organizing my daily schedule.

∞ Goals need to be set so I remain productive.

∞ I could sit home alone all day if I don't do some planning.

A profound sense of gratitude.

∞ I have time to smell the roses.

∞ My days are full.

∞ I have discovered true meaning in my life, what is really important, what really brings me joy.

∞ How full my life is.

∞ How wonderful life is.

∞ I love retirement and have never regretted one moment.

Don't worry, be happy. A great song from Bobby McFerrin comes to mind.

- ∞ "How great it is." "How much fun it is." "How much I like it." Are all heard again and again.
- ∞ How fulfilling it is.
- ∞ I am busy all day long with activities and living an enjoyable life.
- ∞ It's even more fun that I thought it would be.
- ∞ "How much I enjoy it," echoes repeatedly.

Transition surprises

In our survey women commented on the surprises revealed in transitioning out-of-the-paid-work-world. It's easier than you may think, but there are challenges, and it takes time.

It is easier than expected to <u>not</u> look back. "How easy it was," echoed like a rolling thunder cloud.

- ∞ It was dead easy to give up working.
- ∞ How easy it was, as I just continued on with things that I enjoyed and had been involved with during my working days.
- ∞ How easy it was to leave work, not really even missing the social contact, and having plenty of people to do things with.

Being out-of-the-paid-work-world challenges your sense of identity.

∞ Accepting letting go of being in control.

∞ It was difficult at first because I didn't know how to introduce myself; I had to reinvent myself and my identity.

∞ Loss of identity. Lack of recognition. No longer being relevant professionally.

∞ It was hard to adjust initially, in terms of my place in the world.

∞ I miss the validation and recognition that my job provided.

Janet's struggle with identity.
I have always had a business card. It's a form of professional marketing for both me and my company. It extends a sense of legitimacy and identity when making new connections.

When I stepped out-of-the-paid-work-world I didn't have a business card; I wasn't associated with a business anymore. Getting my contact information into the hands of new people I met was now done on scraps of paper, crumpled receipts from the bottom of my purse, or Post-It Notes™. Something was missing.

It went that way for about two years. I accepted it. I thought, "That's just the way it is." Then my husband and I met this delightful gregarious couple at an aviation volunteer event. We connected immediately. The conversation flourished. We would be working together for five days but knew that we'd stay connected. I scrounged around in the bottom of my purse for a pen and an old crumpled receipt to exchange contact information.

In one graceful move she presented me with her card. It wasn't a business card; I guess I would say it was a calling card. It had both her and her husband's contact information and a picture of their boat. How cool! It was their personal brand, not the brand of an organization or business. Their passion was sailing, although their interests spanned many other areas like aviation and writing family history. WOW! This was a revelation. Why couldn't we also have a calling card? Why not!

My husband and I created a calling card when we returned home. Selecting our passion was simple: it's aviation. I love having a calling card. I must admit that I don't use it very often but when I do, I feel a sense of legitimacy and identity. On our card, we are a "we", but your calling card can be your own.

The transition is comfortable.

- ∞ Not missing work.
- ∞ How quickly I adapted to a free open schedule and how much I enjoy it.
- ∞ How fun it is to let go of things that I once thought were so important, and find they really aren't.
- ∞ How little I would miss work.
- ∞ I worked very hard all of my career and expected a massive let down, instead I feel energized.

Ageism can distance us from others.

∞ The range of effect that age has on people I meet; age differentials are treated by others as anything from inconsequential and unimportant to making me feel irrelevant and invisible.

∞ Many "not working" people I meet seem to have some unmet need to seek validation, once they are without a work title; they offer up a list of things they do – volunteer work, taking classes, etc.

∞ I retired from full-time teaching and substitute teach at several schools. Some months were almost full-time. I might have considered going to the in-person schools but, while they do need subs, they identify age and potential health concerns as a reason to not call me.

It is hard to realize that we can create our own ageism. Have you ever heard yourself or someone else say: "When I was your age..." "When I was young..." "I remember when..." "Back in the day..." Statements like these senselessly distance people by age.

Hearing women out-of-the-paid-work-world say: "I'm mostly out-of-the-loop now, but..." "I'm retired, but..." needlessly distances them from people in the work-world when their experience can provide useful information to others more active in the work-world.

Generational tags distance us from others by not valuing the uniqueness of the individual. Except in certain circumstance, try to avoid generational stereotype tags: Boomers, Gen X, Millennials, or Gen Z.

Take time to adjust, adapt, and reinvent.

- ∞ It took me approximately two years to decompress; my schedule and stress level were damaging to my health at the time.
- ∞ It took six months to adjust to a new way of life.
- ∞ It took me some time to adjust to a different lifestyle.
- ∞ It took me more than a year-and-a-half to come down off the daily adrenaline high of working; it seemed like something was missing.
- ∞ Fair to say it was tough going from a high-powered advertising executive to housewife minus kids. Then after the first one or two years how incredible it is to have my day filled with meaningful activities.
- ∞ Within a few months I did not miss going to work each day.

Time surprises

It's not all about the clock. It's about prioritization. The time surprises mentioned by women in our survey respect the clock and recognize that its hands move for them, not just for their work responsibilities.

Time to do what you want.

- ∞ How liberating it is to not work!!!
- ∞ How much I enjoy <u>my</u> free time.
- ∞ I love staying up late and sleeping in.
- ∞ I still get up between 5:00 and 6:00 in the morning.

∞ Taking time for myself.

∞ I can do things more slowly.

∞ Time and energy to exercise, have fun with friends, support my family, and travel.

Time to take care of yourself and turn off the stress.

∞ I began to sleep through the night.

∞ Exercise.

∞ It is more relaxing than I expected.

∞ How much more I sleep now!

∞ A new fitness routine.

∞ Staying fit and vital is a constant undertaking, body parts do get old and energy levels wane.

∞ What it feels like to not be stressed all the time.

∞ The realization of how much a corporate career was affecting both me and my family in terms of time, stress, and overall health.

∞ The joy of relaxed time.

∞ At first it was hard to accept that it's okay to slow down and relax.

Where does the time go? "How fast time goes by," was repeated by many.

∞ How time passes by.

∞ How quickly the days go by.

∞ Is it Friday already?

∞ Even though there is more free time, there are always things that may not get done.

∞ Now so many things can wait until tomorrow!

∞ My schedule fills up.

∞ Not being able to do all the things I want to do, because in having more time to do it, everything takes longer.

"I can do that tomorrow." "Maybe tomorrow." When we are not burdened with a demanding schedule, what is the meaning of tomorrow? Is it the day after today? Or are there many tomorrows? Maybe the word takes on the new context of: "Not today" or "I am not sure when". Talking with Spanish-speaking friends, we laugh in harmony. It is the same for them and the word manaña!

Funny little surprises

∞ The beauty of daylight … after spending so much of my life inside a large office building for a long working day.

∞ How much more often I run the dishwasher.

∞ Having to make my own decisions and maintain routines.

∞ Preparing and eating lunch at home every day.

∞ How much toilet paper I go through now that I am home all the time. (Haha! Didn't we all learn that during the COVID-19 pandemic!)

∞ That the one-hour time change in spring and fall doesn't just affect commuting to and from work but changes my whole perspective on the world.

∞ Comfortable clothes.

∞ Doing everything with my husband, no more divide and conquer, our daily routines are tightly

197

intertwined – we grocery shop and workout together.

∞ Choosing to read a book all day, rather than doing something else.

Challenging surprises

Changes in life bring challenge, both good and bad. Anticipate them. Change will affect finances, interpersonal relationships, routines, and more. Many of these challenges have been discussed previously, except for one: relocation.

About one million people in North America move every year when they are out-of-the-paid-work-world, according to NorthAmerican.com. Relocation can be for pleasure, health, financial, or family reasons. A few people may even build their "dream house".

Moving.

∞ Moving took some adjustment, people were immediately welcoming but it took about three years to really feel part of the new community, but within five years we are the community.

∞ I moved to a new area without school-aged children; it took fresh creativity and effort to make friends and engage in the new community.

∞ Moving wasn't as traumatic as I had envisioned.

Building a house.

> ∞ How trying it is to build a custom home, but I would have done so anyway.

Meeting people.

> ∞ I relocated for financial reasons and have been surprised at how difficult it is to meet people.

> ∞ I take classes, do volunteer work, joined two book clubs, and belong to two ancestry societies, but it's all women – I miss discussions with men too.

Surprising volunteer work

There are volunteer activities to suit every interest, if volunteering is on your priority list. A tremendous body of information is available about volunteer work in any phase of school, work, or private life, and in any number of capacities.

In our survey, community involvement was ranked number-three in importance by women in every work relationship. For women in the thick-of-it, it's what they look forward to. For the women working on my-own-terms, it's what they most enjoy doing in their "not working" time. For those out-of-the-paid-work-world, community involvement is a multi-faceted source of enjoyment.

If you are (or were) an active volunteer during your work years, you can expect that commitment to volunteer activities to continue. If you have never really been an active volunteer, volunteering may or may not be in your future. It's your age of freedom, so you decide if, where, and what volunteer activities might fit into your life. You can also drop in and drop out of volunteer work; it is optional.

The joy of volunteering.

∞ I finally have time for volunteer activities that really interest me.

∞ I enjoy all the community volunteer work.

∞ The satisfaction I get from volunteering; I can choose the level of involvement and type of organization depending on the focus of their work.

The struggle.

∞ I have found it hard to volunteer in places I enjoy.

∞ How I can't say no to volunteer work, when they ask.

∞ Volunteering also includes the amount of time I spend helping family members.

The time commitment.

∞ I became involved in too many non-profit organizations as a volunteer and had to learn to say no and allocate my time more carefully.

∞ So many community organizations are in desperate need of volunteers.

∞ How little time I have for fun now – I volunteer a lot, maybe too much.

Meeting amazing people.

∞ Through community volunteer work I met so many highly educated and accomplished people that I wouldn't have met otherwise.

∞ My women friends multiplied as I found others that were volunteering and did not work.

∞ I can replace the relationships from work with those from my activities and enjoy them even more.

Non-profits need help.

∞ On the whole, non-profits are poorly run; it's hard not to step in and get the place organized.

No surprises

No surprises come to mind for just a few of those out-of-the-paid-work-world. "Life is better, no regrets. Nothing. Can't think of anything. No surprises. None. Nothing in particular."

∞ ∞ ∞

It is interesting to peek into being out-of-the-paid-work-world. The Surprises were a thoughtful and contemplative look at some of the unexpected elements beyond the work world. The answers to the Magic Question provide understanding of how to approach and prepare for it, if you choose to head out-of-the-paid-work-world.

Chapter 8

What the Heck To Do Now?

So, what's the plan?

Living an ordinary life is not enough. Ordinary doesn't describe your professional life. So, as you look at what's next, ordinary is just not in the equation.

What does your "next" look like? Now, it's your turn to participate in the *Age of Freedom*, not just read and contemplate.

What's "next" will be different for each of us. It will vary based on where you are in your relationship to work: if you are in the thick-of-it, working on my-own-terms, or out-of-the-paid-work-world.

We could simply tell you that it's your choice in the age of freedom. Wash our hands and be done with it. But somehow that just doesn't feel right.

Satisfaction with our career and professional life gives us a strong emotional foundation and stability. It offers the ability to leverage our skills and talents and apply those in unique ways.

For Janice, as she moved from being in the thick-of-it to working on my-own-terms, she is grateful to successfully leverage her leadership skills as a coach in her consulting practice. Her greatest reward is being able to give back and mentor younger women who are at the beginning of their leadership journey.

As Janet moved from working on my-own-terms to being out-of-the-paid-work-world, fulfillment comes from inspiring others. Whether it is inspiring people embarking on new careers, the next generation of aviation enthusiasts, or people to author their stories.

In *Chapter 4: Happiness, Wellness, and Healthcare,* we introduced the National Institute of Wellness' six-dimensional model. As you are determining what's next bring these six interconnected dimensions into your plan. They individually and collectively contribute to a healthy life.

1. *Environmental well-being.* Contributing to your environment and community, building better living, working, and social spaces.
2. *Mental wellness.* Enriching life through work and its interconnectedness to living and playing.

3. *Spiritual strength.* Developing belief systems, values, and creating a worldview.
4. *Physical vitality.* The benefits of regular physical activity, healthy eating habits, strength and vitality as well as personal responsibility, self-care and knowing when to seek medical attention.
5. *Emotional security.* Self-esteem, self-control, and determination as a sense of direction.
6. *Social connectivity.* Creative and stimulating mental activities and sharing your gifts with others.

As you ponder, "What the heck will I do now?" take skills from your career that are consistent with your personal values, interests, and beliefs. These will enable you to create an enriching and exciting new chapter, no matter what you choose to do. Each of us has unique gifts and talents that can be put to work in meaningful and rewarding ways – full-time, part-time, or on your own time.

We have a formula to figure out what the heck comes next. It's not all analytical, left-brained math. It requires creativity, artistry, and right-brain engagement. Think of it as a personal management theorem. You will also find some worksheets for self-guided exploration in *Appendix 2: Worksheets for What the Heck To Do Now.* Read on and we will demystify our personal management formula for you.

$$CV + PI + DP = IAP$$

Our personal management formula

Core Values (CV)

What defines you? Core values are the fundamental principles that guide you, your inner strength, and your conduct. For example, it could be authenticity, compassion, dependability, kindness, fearlessness, honesty, loyalty, optimism, pragmatism, or any number of other things that make you uniquely you.

What causes or basic rights do you believe in? Core values are essential convictions that underpin your determination and your actions. This can be almost anything: animal rights, charity, community development, death with dignity, education, environment, equality, historic preservation, religion, support for the arts, or other key principles.

We think it's helpful to write them down. The act of writing them down has you explore, think about, evaluate, and commit to them.

If you are not sure how to approach this or where to start, begin with a recent personal event that was high impact. Examine how you handled it, what decisions you made and actions you took. Write down the values that guided your judgment and behavior. Or you may prefer to start with your resume and examine the critical underlying standards, ethics, and tenets that have guided your career.

Next step away from the event or your resume to think about people you most admire in history, at work, at play, in reading, and in your family. Why and how do they inspire you? Consider their words of wisdom, actions, and guiding principles that have inspired, strengthened, and assisted you in your unique journey through life. As an example, you can see some of our core values in the quotes we selected for this book and our shared personal stories.

As you compare the results, central themes will emerge. These will allow you to identify and select your top core values.

Connecting with our core values is important. It helps us understand the foundation that our professional and personal lives are built on.

Personal Investigation (PI)

Next, it's time to examine where you are and where you want to go from here. You are doing a personal investigation (PI) of what's next. If this were a research grant or public service project, you would be the principal investigator, assuming full responsibility for the research study or project. This is much the same. Your research study or project is YOU.

Your personal investigation can help elevate your current work-relationship to the next level or prepare you for a transition to another.

PI for those in the thick-of-it

If you are in the thick-of-it, examine the top three things that you want to define your next chapter. Pull from the ideas below or create your own.

- Re-engage with work in a new way
- Re-prioritize work-life balance
- Take on a new level of responsibility
- Find a new career opportunity
- Start a new business
- Simplify life and work
- Focus on health
- Build a more complete financial plan

Take each idea and build on it. Again, we recommend writing it down - use smartphone notes, a bullet journal, Word document, or whatever works for you. As an example in the middle of the idea stack above, is "a new career opportunity" which may have key steps similar to these.

1. Assess your current career goals. Are you satisfied where you are?
2. What risks would you encounter if you left your current job? (Are the risks financial, job level, or something else.)
3. Are you willing to move out of your comfort zone to something you have never tried?
4. What motivates you in your current job?
5. What are you willing to give up?

PI if you are working on my-own-terms

If you are currently working on my-own-terms, your investigation will look at a different set of factors. Develop your own list, work with these, or check out *Appendix 2* for additional ideas.

- Change how you work
- Launch a new business
- Shift to self-employment or working for others
- Expand self-realization and self-understanding
- Step out-of-the-paid-work-world or back into the thick-of-it
- Re-examine "your terms" – those seven W-H questions
- Purpose and fulfillment

Take time to examine each area. Ask yourself the tough questions. Perhaps even ask yourself some questions that you hadn't faced before. This can be a great time for a tune up to get your internal engine running at optimal performance.

1. What flexibility do you have in how you work today? What flexibility do you want?
2. What would it take for you to change your work style for the better?
3. What are the positive aspects that you enjoy? What things do you least enjoy?
4. What are you most worried about?

PI out-of-the-paid-work-world.

If you are out-of-the-paid-work-world, is there a "next"? Yes, there is. We can refine and redefine ourselves at any time. So, what does your "next" look like? Maybe you are already doing it. No matter what the "it" is, could it be done differently or better? Here are some ideas for you to explore.

- Refocus community involvement
- Tune up your investment management approach
- Travel in a different way
- Rebalance work-leisure-family life
- Expand involvement in more volatile issues: social, political, economic, ecological, other
- Rejoin the paid work-world
- Attain new skills and learning

Here are some self-examination questions to test yourself. Feel free to add your own.

1. Are you living the life of your hopes and dreams? What is fulfilling those hopes and dreams, and what is not?
2. If you could turn back the clock, what would you do differently? What would you not change?
3. What would you do if fear was not a factor, and you could not fail?
4. What are you most grateful for?
5. Are you truly proud of who you are? Why or why not?

This personal investigation (PI) is an opportunity to test yourself. Yes, it's a test, like a student back in school. Taking tests can be unpleasant and stressful. However, tests are also beneficial and help you learn. In school, testing is an assessment of knowledge attained. Here, your PI test is an examination of where you are and where you want to go from here.

Core values (CV) plus your personal investigation (PI) is what's most meaningful to you in your next steps. If you are not growing and learning, you are shrinking and withering – you don't want to go there.

Development Plan (DP)

As professionals, we have all had some sort of development plan. Some are more structured than others, but we have all had one. A professional development plan is a roadmap to further our career through building skills, knowledge, and strategy needed to achieve our goals. It is a structured approach to succeed in our chosen field.

Your development plan may look similar to the table below.

Goal/ Target Objective	Action Steps & Resources	Measure Success
Keep current	• Workshop • Online course • Self-study	• Course completion • Keep up & ahead
Improve and expand expertise	• Read key books • Investigate • Find a mentor	• Behavior changes • Improve skills
Continued education	• Attend lectures • Research • Expand contacts	• Knowledge upgrade • New best practice
Add related experience	• New functions • Leadership • Examine new things	• Apply new skills • Evaluate existing process

If your professional development plan is only in your head, it's time to put it on paper, in your smartphone, or on your computer. Now is a good time to prepare one. It will help you succeed to that next level of professional or personal achievement.

We want you to add a personal dimension to your development plan. Take your core values plus your personal investigation (CV+PI) and make it a work-and-life development plan (DP). Look at the table above again, this time through a personal lens. The same key factors apply to your personal life: there are goals to be sought, resources available, and success to be attained.

Your professional and personal development plan is a way to plan ahead. It will help you anticipate what internal and external resources that will provide the support needed to attain your goals and discover your "new me".

The development plan (DP) added to your core values and personal investigation yields a design for action and resources that will help you achieve your goals.

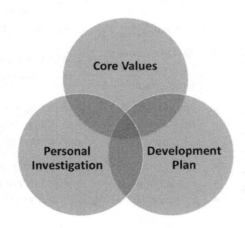

There is a logical relationship between the three key elements: core values, personal investigation, and development plan. Knowingly or unknowingly these three elements are what has helped us, and you, become successful professional women. Apply these three elements to answer your question of: "What the heck to do now?"

Our personal management formula has taken shape. All three elements are necessary for a balanced approach.

Core values plus personal investigation (CV+PI) will feel comfortable. But without a development plan there is no sense of direction. Your essential principals are clear but there is no action to attain them.

Personal investigation plus a development plan (PI+DP) will be exciting with a powerful sense of direction. But may leave you unfulfilled or blindsided by bad organizational behavior.

Core values plus a development plan (CV+DP) will feel comfortable and satisfying. But you'll feel empty and useless: asking yourself: "What's the point?"

All three elements are essential to developing a satisfying, rewarding, actionable, and enjoyable answer to what's next (CV+PI+DP). It's your "what's next", and no one else's.

- "What's next" may not involve change but further dedication to where you are and what you are currently doing.

- "What's next" could involve dramatic change into something completely new and different.
- Or it may be an adjustment or modification to the path you are already on.

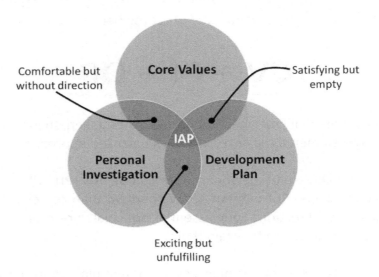

Let's explore the powerful result that bringing all three key elements together can yield. It's the intersection of activity and purpose.

Intersection of Activity and Purpose (IAP)

Meaningful purpose is defined by you, not by someone or something else. It can be intensified by powerful external forces like business, politics, the economy, religion, culture, media, or even a pandemic. It can be affected by more subtle things like personal relationships, social influence, peers or where you live. True purpose and significance come from within. You own it. It is your own purposeful sense of meaning.

As professional women, our company, industry, customers, partners, and functional responsibilities shape meaning and purpose for us. These are highly varied and specialized depending on what role we fulfill in healthcare, high tech, education, consulting, manufacturing, or public sector.

In our personal lives, our family, friends, and interests shape meaning and purpose for us. These are unique, subjective, and intimately intertwined with who we are.

Activity and action are dependent upon the job to be done. Whether it is personal or professional, if something needs to be done, we will approach it with resolve and determination: initiate, plan, design, do, test, and track performance. It is the same at work as with our personal lives, although work has more structure and time constraints wrapped around it.

Purpose and activity are intimately linked in every aspect of life.

Without purpose, activity is meaningless. It is being busy without accomplishing anything. It is that caged-hamster-on-a-running-wheel kind of busy that never goes anywhere. Without purpose, planning and preparation is ineffective or not required. A GPS without a destination may know where it is, but it won't get you anywhere. Without purpose, goals or points would not be scored in football, tennis, baseball, or ice hockey.

Without action, purpose is unfulfilled: squandered and rendered useless. Even great thinkers, philosophers, and religious leaders must bring their thoughts into action. If their thoughts are not written down or shared with another person, they are lost forever. Forgotten. Seeds that never get planted; seeds that never have an opportunity to grow.

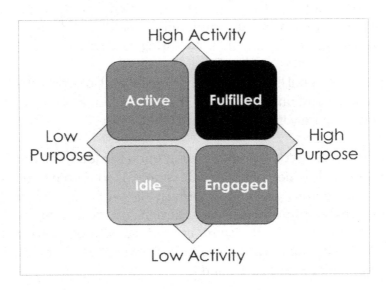

The intersection of activity and purpose (IAP) is a transformative guide. Purpose and activity can orient you. In *Chapter 4: Happiness, Wellness and Healthcare*, Juanita T told us her story, here she shows how the intersection of activity and purpose works for her.

> *Juanita T's IAP reaffirmed her commitment.*
> In the thick-of-it, I was a critical care nurse for forty years, working in the intensive care unit. Today on my-own-terms, I am a palliative care nurse. I help patients and their families achieve the best possible

quality of life right up until the end, with a main focus on comfort for all.

Examining the formula and applying it helped me to reaffirm that I was in the right place, doing exactly what I should be doing. My formula looks like this:

- ✓ My CV is kindness and ethical work.
- ✓ My PI is purpose and fulfillment -- I want people to die in a dignified manner.
- ✓ My DP is improving and expanding my expertise; this is a new specialty for me.

I am very fulfilled by what I do.

Where are you? "I'm idle and bored." Or you might say, "I'm active but it feels like that caged-hamster-on-a-running-wheel kind of busy." Where do you want to go? Maybe you want to engage. Discover or seek a higher purpose.

The intersection of activity and purpose can apply at any time in our lives. Take a self-guided tour of your IAP, check out *Appendix 2: Worksheets for What the Heck to do Now* . The intersection of activity and purpose emerges as we look deeply at how women change their relationship to the work-world. Choose where you want to be. Set off in a new direction. Embrace a different level of effectiveness. As Ralph Waldo Emerson says, "Life is a journey, not a destination."

$$CV \; + \; PI \; + \; DP \; = \; IAP$$

| Core Values | + | Personal Investigation | + | Development Plan | = | Intersection of Activity & Purpose |

Your core values combined with personal investigation and a development plan yield your personal intersection of activity and purpose. Go for it. Adjust it along the way. Never stop striving.

Thank you for joining us for this journey.

J-and-J

About the Authors

Janice and Janet

Janet A. Gregory is cofounder and principal of KickStart Alliance (www.KickStartall.com), a consulting firm dedicated to connecting clients with their customers. She worked as an independent consultant for seventeen years providing strategy in business development and sales planning. She is now working in an advisory capacity with a few select clients.

Janet has over twenty-five years of corporate experience in Silicon Valley. Every minute of those twenty-five years in the thick of her career were exhilarating. Janet looks back across those years with great memories of the growth, success, and conquests, as well as the poignant learning experiences through the struggles, failures, and losses. Her entire career has been based in Silicon Valley and in some ways, she feels she grew up along with Silicon Valley.

The first start-up was in the THICK of the thick-of-it in Silicon Valley. Janet was a member of the founding executive team. After that Janet began working on her own terms, consulting. Within two years, she co-founded the successful consulting firm KickStart Alliance, which is still thriving today. Janet embraced the freedom to work independently with the same energy and commitment that defined her in the corporate world. She thrived on the deep learning that accompanied consulting work.

There was an intermission where Janet jumped back into the corporate world, joining one of her clients as their Vice President of Sales on the turn-around team. When she wrapped up that role, Janet had the freedom to rejoin the consulting firm she co-founded.

Fast forward through seventeen years of full-time consulting, Janet admits to reinventing herself and leaving the paid work-world at age sixty-seven ... except for an occasional consulting assignment that interests her.

Janet has transited three distinctly different relationships with the work-world, nimbly moving back and forth between them. This is the power possessed in the *Age of Freedom:* the power to change trajectory and speed, and alter course in your life's work.

Janet thrives personally, whether it's piloting her own plane, mentoring young aviators, skiing, hiking, or giving back to her community. The *Age of Freedom* is Janet's fourth book. All of her publications have been co-authored as she feels the power of collaboration achieves a better result.

Janet and Janice, Whistler

Janice Hulse founded Global Directions in 2012 after a successful career in Asia Pacific that spanned fourteen years. In 2012, she returned to North America and began her consultancy career by partnering with KickStart Alliance and The Aspire Group. Her consultancy work focused on technology sales mentorship, which she continues to do for a select group of clients and partners.

Janice's professional experience began thirty-four years ago in San Francisco, where she cut her teeth in sales with a variety of technology start-ups. She was in a nascent industry that was only starting to get its foothold within the business sector. She experienced many ups and downs. Some start-ups never actually started and others were quickly acquired or left behind. Even so, it was an exhilarating time. Janice left her mark as a top sales professional in a sector where women were few and far between.

Janice is a constant learner. She looks life right in the eye and absorbs as much as possible—both personally and professionally. She faces the unknown. While in the thick of her career, she embarked on her next journey—taking her and her family to Asia. She led a company's Asia Pacific division and oversaw its merger into a new global operation following the company's acquisition.

From there, she joined a Fortune-100 technology company while still in Asia. She led regional teams in business development and sales for emerging markets, as well as channel and partner operations.

After fourteen years living abroad, Janice knew that it was time to move physically and professionally. She wanted to begin a new endeavor on her own terms. Janice reconnected with Janet—whose consulting work was thriving—and they worked together on several projects. Janice used her experience in Asia to build new partnerships with clients on a global level.

While Janice is working on her own terms; she continues to give back and use her experience by mentoring and volunteering in her community. From time to time, a consulting opportunity crosses her desk—giving her a further opportunity to use her experience and insights.

Janice's passion is in the mountains. Her zest for the outdoors took hold after living for many years in dense urban areas. She speaks three languages, dabbles in watercolor, and loves to get her hands in the dirt while gardening.

This is Janice's first book. *The Age of Freedom* speaks to her own career and personal journey. Through this book and her own experience, Janice joins the many voices of women who made this book possible.

Appendix

Appendix 1: Strength of the Voices

Over 650 women, ages 40 to 80, from North America and around the globe responded to our survey. Surveys were anonymous, allowing for open and honest responses. The book analyzes and describes the responses, prioritizing them. Here are some of the statistics behind the observations made in the book.

If you are looking for data associated with something specific, here's a table to help you find it.

Table of Contents for Appendix 1:

The surveys

The original vision was to write a book for and about professional women retiring. What we learned from the survey dramatically changed our original concept.

Then, in the midst of writing and analyzing the responses, the global COVID-19 pandemic hit, which changed the concept yet again. We sent out a COVID supplement survey in late 2020 to the original survey respondents.

Nothing makes me more nervous
than people who say, "It can't happen here."
Anything can happen anywhere,
given the right circumstances.
Margaret Atwood, Canadian poet, novelist,
teacher, environmental activist, and inventor.
Quote from a 2015 lecture to West Point cadets

The original survey had forty-five questions, but no one had to answer more than twenty-six questions due to survey branches. It took an average of ten minutes to complete the survey.

The first thirteen questions were answered by all survey participants. Based on responses to those initial questions, respondents were directed to answer additional questions targeted to their work status:

1. Working full-time.
2. Working but not necessarily full-time, could be moving in and out of the work-world or established in a part-time career.
3. Fully retired.

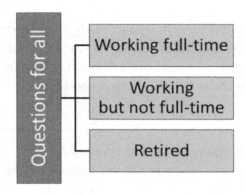

The first thirteen questions for all were closed-end questions that could be easily analyzed statistically. In the questions targeted to their work status, there were both closed- and open-ended questions. The open-ended questions allowed for free-form, complex responses. The book compiles and analyzes these free-form responses.

We didn't realize that our initial survey was "assumptive" and several people in the free-form response told us that in no uncertain terms. This quote from one woman sums it up quite clearly.

> "This survey makes lots of assumptions about retirement. It assumes at a certain age you want to retire, that just isn't the case. The bias leapt out of the survey. Disappointing to reinforce the ageist view held by society, particularly for women."

*The truth, however ugly in itself, is always curious
and beautiful to seekers after it.
Everything must be taken into account.
If the fact will not fit the theory – let the theory go.*
Agatha Christie, English Author

We listened and we learned.

We learned that a professional woman's relationship with the work-world is not age related. Women in all age groups work full-time, part-time, or have stepped out-of-the-paid-work-world.

We learned that a professional woman's relationship with the work-world is not linear or one directional. Traditional thinking was that work moves from full-time to not-working **or** full-time to part-time, then on to not-working. But we find that is NOT necessarily the case. Professional women continuously redefine themselves. They change their relationship with the work-world to suit their needs. The work-life balance can shift at any time for any number of reasons.

The freedom and flexibility of professional women to continuously redefine their relationship with the work-world became even more apparent with the COVID-19 pandemic.

We learned from carefully studying and analyzing the responses that "retirement" is an old, outdated concept. We chose to minimize the use of the word "retirement" in the book because it carries too much baggage and preconceptions. Women's relationship to the work-world in our book has been defined as:

1. **In the thick-of-it**, fully engaged in the work-world and working full-time.
2. **Working on my-own-terms**, working but typically not full-time or moving in and out of the work-world.
3. **Out-of-the-paid-work-world**, still engaged but fully retired, without the baggage.

I will not be "famous", "great".
I will go on adventuring, changing, opening my mind and my eyes, refusing to be stamped and stereotyped.
The thing is to free one's self:
to let it find its dimensions, not to be impeded.
Virginia Woolf, English Author

Professional women answering our survey

Work relationship. Professional women are the masters of their own destiny. The women responding to our survey declared their current relationship with the work-world as:

- **In the thick-of-it:** 48% are fully engaged with career, working full-time but may also be working on their-own-terms.
- **Working on my-own-terms:** 24% are being paid for the work performed, but not necessarily working full-time.
- **Out-of-the-paid-work-world**, still actively engaged but money is not the prime motivator.

Relationship to Work-World

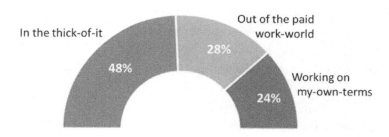

In the thick-of-it

Out of the paid work-world

28%

48%

Working on my-own-terms

24%

Functional Role. Women in our survey span every aspect of the business world from individual contributor to business owner. Nearly two-thirds are managers and executives.

- 37% supervisors, managers, or directors
- 31% executive (VP) or senior executive (CXO)
- 17% business owners
- 15% individual contributors

37%	31%	17%	15%
Managers	Executives	Business Owners	Individual Contributors

Industry. As professional women, those responding to our survey contribute in all industry sectors.

- Education 14.6%
- Healthcare 14.3%
- Consulting 12.4%
- Financial Services 9.7%
  (incl. Insurance, Real Estate, Banking)
- Manufacturing 7.2%
- High Tech 6.4%
- Essential Public Services 5%
  (incl. public utilities)
- Public Sector 5%
  (incl. Government)
- Other 26%
  - Retail or Wholesale trade
  - Tourism
    (incl. Hospitality)
  - Construction
  - Agriculture, Forestry, Fishing

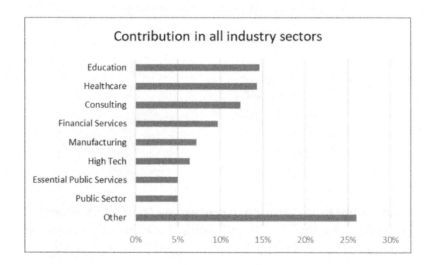

Functional Role. Women work in every role regardless of their profession: customer facing, teaching, management, human relations, finance, operations, technical, healthcare and production.

Developing. Professional women tell us that they are flourishing, yet still developing and growing. There are goals that have been successfully achieved and more that they strive to reach in their personal TPA, top professional achievement.

- 41% feel satisfied that they have successfully reached their TPA.
- 59% continue to expand their professional goals.
    - 30% have goals ahead to reach their TPA.
    - 29% have reached TPA with potential to progress further.

Flourishing and Developing

Change of work relationship. Leaving full-time work is an option, but only <u>if and when the time is right</u>.

- 88% will leave full-time work based on personal choice.
    - They will choose when and if to leave the work-world for private or personal reasons of family, health, life balance, or other reasons.

Choice drives change

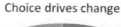

- 12% will leave the work-world because it is required.
  - For 8% it is compulsory/mandatory (5%) or suggested/recommended (3%) by company, occupation or age.
  - 4% leave work out of necessity for reasons of family, health, or something else.

We were not surprised to see that personal choice was central to the decision to change the relationship with the work-world. What did surprise us was the 88%. If you had asked us before the survey, we expected the balance to be 70/30 or 80/20 at most. We thought that more people were driven by mandated work change.

The impact of COVID-19 may have shifted this balance with more recommendations to leave work due to company down-sizing, insolvency, or other economic reasons.

I am no bird; and no net ensnares me:
I am a free human being with an
independent will.
Charlotte Brontë, English novelist, *Jane Eyre*

Residence. Women responding to our survey mainly live in North America.

- 88% are North American respondents, primarily from the U.S. and Canada.
- 12% are from other points on the globe: 5% Asia-Pacific, 3% Europe, 3% Australia and New Zealand, 1% Latin America, and none from Africa.

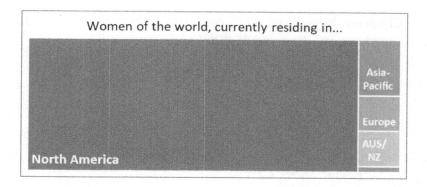

Proud and resourceful

Education. Professional women responding to our survey are smart, practical, and imaginative. Certification and educational degrees don't necessarily define intellect, smarts, or wits.

- 53% have advanced degrees: Master's Degree (43%), PhD, or other specialized degree (10%).
- 34% have an undergraduate degree.
- 13% have a high school education, some college, and/or specialized vocational training.

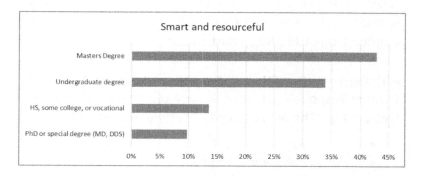

Children. In our survey two-thirds of the women told us they have children and 35% did not.

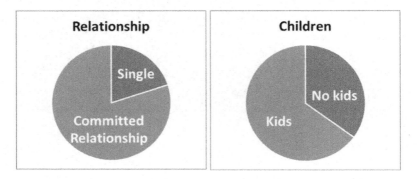

Relationships. More than three-quarters (78%) are in some sort of committed relationship: married, in partnership, or comparable, along with Janet and Janice. This, obviously, means that 22% live independently, as singles or separated: widowed, divorced, or never married.

Age. "How old would you be if you didn't know how old you are?" asked Satchel Paige, professional baseball pitcher.

As women, we don't typically describe ourselves by age. "Sorry, but that's none of your business!" We sought out women who were accomplished in their careers, asking women from 40 to 80 to participate.

Although you might not typically reveal your age, the women responding to our survey did share this personal fact with us. The average age of survey respondents is 61.

- 8% are younger than 50.
- 34% are between 50 and 59.
- 42% are between 60 and 69.
- 15% are age 70 or better.

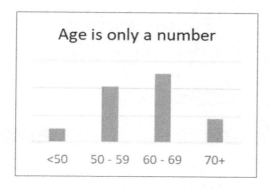

Age is not the determining factor. Our relationship to the work-world is our choice. We determine the best fit for our own unique life and lifestyle.

Work relationship and age. If you are curious as to how many other women in your age range share the same work-world relationship with you, the chart below examines this question. The age mix in each work-related category is not particularly surprising. This chart normalizes the quantity of responses in each work-related category to 100%, providing a fair comparison of the percent of women in each age range.

Placing us in the chart below, we are both in the light pearl 60 to 69 age range. Janice is working on my-own-terms, joining more than half (58%) of the women working on my-own-terms that are between 60 and 69. Janet is out-of-the-paid-work-world and finds a similar percent of women (57%) in her 60 to 69 age range.

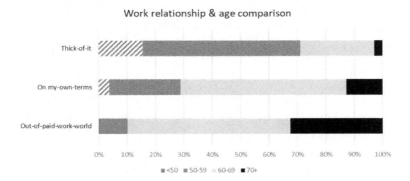

Another way to think about this is if Janet was in a room with one-hundred women who are also out-of-the-paid-work-world, fifty-seven women (including her) would be in their 60's, eleven would be in their 50's or younger (pattern and dark pearl), and thirty-two women would be age 70 or better (jet-black). Similarly, if Janice was in another room with one-hundred of her peers working on my-own-terms, four women would be under age 50 (pattern), twenty-five would be in their 50s (dark pearl), fifty-eight women (including Janice) would be in their 60s (light pearl), and thirteen would be age 70 or better (jet-black).

Describing life beyond work

In *Chapter 2: Voices of the Age of Freedom,* we explored the "new me" and the "comparative" in depth. Those two descriptors express the opinion of over 80% of the women responding to our survey.

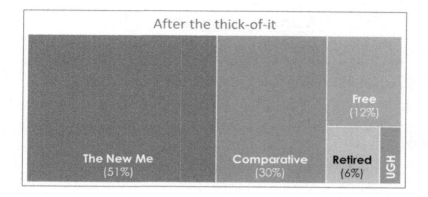

To feed your analytical and methodical left-brain, below is the detail behind each of the categories. The agreement across the three work-relationships is astounding: compare the Total Average column across the three groups.

Category	Total Average ⬇	The thick-of-it	On my-own terms	Not in Paid-work-world
The New Me	*51%*	53%	44%	55%
Comparative	*30%*	25%	36%	28%
Free	*12%*	13%	11%	13%
Retired	*6%*	6%	6%	5%
UGH	*2%*	4%	3%	0%
	100%	*100%*	*100%*	*100%*

Women in the thick-of-it

Women in the thick of their careers are working full-time and are the master of their own destiny.

Fight for the things that you care about,
but do it in a way that will lead others to join you.
Ruth Bader Ginsberg,
American lawyer and Supreme Court Justice

Future work plans

Women in the thick-of-it see options for their future work plans.

- 55% want to work part-time or work on their-own-terms.
  - o 40% will continue working in the same field but scale back on the hours.
  - o 15% want to continue working part-time but in a different field.
- 29% look forward to NOT working and want to do something different. Of those, 11% would change something immediately, if it were possible.
- 15% are fully engaged and want to continue working full-time. With 1% of those wanting to continue full-time work, but in a different field.

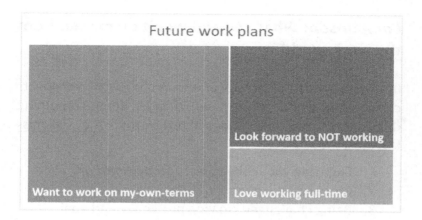

Age. The average age of women in the thick-of-it, responding to our survey, is 57.

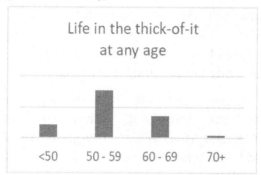

- 16% are younger than 50. But this represents 86% of all survey respondents younger than 50.
- 55% are between 50 and 59, which is the largest number of respondents in this age group.
- 26% are between 60 and 69.
- 3% are age 70 or better.

Comparison: What will and won't be missed from the work-world

In the thick-of-it, professional women enjoy many aspects of the work-world. When they consider doing something different, the top three things that they think they will miss the most are:

1. Engaging with colleagues. *Top three for all.*
2. Meeting new people.
3. Being challenged, solving problems, and goal setting. *Top three for all.*

The three things that they will NOT miss are:

- Organized schedule and routines. *Bottom three for all.*
- Business travel. *Bottom three for all.*
- Managing people and/or process.

The table below shows the stack rankings compared to women in the thick-of-it. What will be missed: 1=High★★★ and 10=Low♥♥♥. Women out-of-the-paid-work-world tell us what they actually do miss (1-3) and what they don't (8-10).

I will miss...	Avg	Thick-of-it ↓	My-own-terms	Out of paid work-world
Engaging with colleagues	1	★★★1★★★	★★2★★	★★★1★★★
Meeting new people	3	★★2★★	5	5
Being challenged	2	★3★	★★★1★★★	★★2★★
Professional recognition	6	4	♥♥♥10♥♥♥	★3★
Business goals	4	5	★3★	6
Staying relevant	5	6	4	4
Work tools	7	7	♥8♥	7
Schedule & routines	8	♥8♥	6	♥♥9♥♥
Travel for business	10	♥♥9♥♥	♥♥9♥♥	♥♥♥10♥♥♥
Managing	9	♥♥♥10♥♥♥	7	♥8♥

Rattling around in the middle of the stack ranking for women in the thick-of-it are four things that they expect to miss from their work life:

4. Professional recognition. *This is dramatically different from women on my-own-terms who rank professional recognition dead last #10.*
5. Business goals and set business purpose. *Another dramatic difference with women working on my-own-terms who rank this number-three and will be missed.*
6. Staying relevant on business and industry issues. *Mid-stack for all.*
7. Work tool and resource accessibility. *Mid-stack for all.*

Women on my-own-terms

Women working on my-own-terms design their own destiny. They are paid for the work they do, but they may not necessarily be working full-time.

The right way of doing things is whatever happens to be working for you. Some people have to start at the beginning and go through in order until they get to the end. Other people are making pieces and then arranging them. Some people like to … get it perfect before they move on. There are no surefire rules that are going to work for everyone.

Toni Morrison
American novelist and 1993 Nobel Prize Winner

Age. The average age of women working on my-own-terms is 63.

- 4% are younger than 50.
- 25% are between 50 and 59.
- 58% are between 60 and 69, which is the largest number of respondents in this age group.
- 13% are age 70 or better.

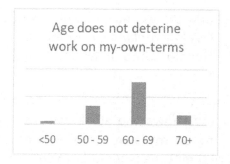

Comparison: Pleasures of non-working time

Working on my-own-terms affords professional women the opportunity to balance their time and priorities between work and non-work activities. As they compare themselves to their colleagues, they agree that travel is a priority, which amplified during COVID restrictions. When not working, the things that women on my-own-terms <u>most enjoy</u> are:

1. Relationships. *Strengthening relationships with family and friends.*
2. Travel. *Top three for all in the original survey and the number-one thing missed during COVID pandemic restrictions.*
3. Health & Fitness. *Improving sleep and general fitness. Access to fitness centers, massage, and in-person workout classes were highly missed with pandemic restrictions.*

As women on my-own-terms compare to their colleagues, there was general agreement that adventure and professional-related activities are at the bottom of the list. Living and working on my-own-terms, professional women spend <u>the least</u> time with:

- Adventure related activities. *Bottom of the list for all.*

- Doing new things and stepping out of their comfort zone. *This low ranking surprised us.*
- Professional-related activities. *Bottom of all three lists.*

The table below shows the stack rankings compared to women working on my-own-terms. Having the ability to balance where their time is spent between working and not working, this is how they spend their "not working" time. 1=High★ ★ ★ and 10=Low👎👎👎.

My "not working" time is spent ...	Avg	My-own-terms ↓	Thick-of-it	Out of paid work-world
Relationships	2	★ ★ ★1★ ★ ★	4	★ ★2★ ★
Travel	1	★ ★2★ ★	★ ★ ★1★ ★ ★	★ ★ ★1★ ★ ★
Health & Fitness	3	★3★	★ ★2★ ★	5
Personal Development	6	4	5	6
Hobbies	5	5	6	★3★
Community	4	6	★3★	4
Creative	7	7	👎👎9👎👎	7
Adventure	9	👎8👎	👎8👎	👎👎9👎👎
New things	8	👎👎9👎👎	7	👎8👎
Professional	10	👎👎👎10👎👎👎	👎👎👎10👎👎👎	👎👎👎10👎👎👎

Women working on my-own-terms have a very different perspective on where things fall in the middle of the stack.

4. Personal development in learning and interests. *Mid-stack for all.*
5. Hobbies. *For women out-of-the-paid-work-world, hobbies rank number-three near the top of their list.*
6. Community involvement. *Quite a bit higher on the list for women in the thick-of-it (#3) and those out-of-the-paid-work-world (#4).*
7. Creative or art activities (painting, writing, theater, music, etc.). *Sits at the bottom of the middle stack for all, a bit surprising to us. But with the impact of the COVID*

pandemic, everyone missed live performing arts and movie theaters.

The graph below shows these same stack rankings compared to women working on my-own-terms, displayed in the first jet-black bar. What women in the thick-of-it look forward to when they have "not working" time is displayed in the middle grey bar. What women out-of-the-paid-work-world actually do spend their time on is the third patterned bar.

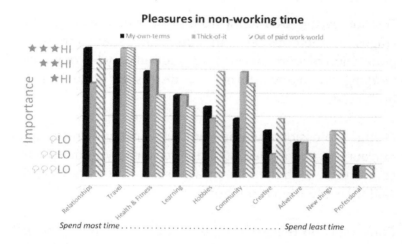

Pleasures in non-working time

Financial stability

Women who are comfortable with their financial stability are more likely to work on my-own-terms. Conversely, women that are not comfortable with their financial position will probably remain in a structured work environment with more predictable income; remaining in the thick-of-it and in the employment of others.

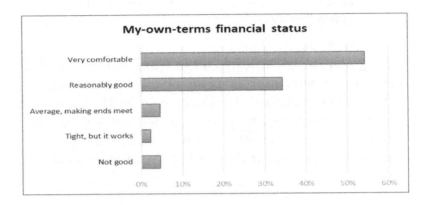

Our survey targeted input from professional women at all stages of their career and <u>does not</u> reflect the entire population of women. Our survey found only 5% of women working on my-own-terms are distressed about making ends meet.

Of the professional women working on my-own-terms in our survey, more than 80% are reasonably good or very comfortable with their financial position, and very few (5%) said their situation is not good.

Conversely, in the general population of women, a report from the Canadian Imperial Bank of Commerce (CIBC) states that 62% of women worry about their finances. Younger women (18-34) are the most concerned, followed by those aged 35-54, with women over 55 being the least worried. Similarly, according to NBC News, an American news organization, 45% of women age 41-56 are discouraged about their financial condition.

Women out-of-the-paid-work-world

Women who have stepped out-of-the-paid-work-world are still actively engaged, but not for income.

---

*We turn not older with years
but newer every day.*
Emily Dickinson
American poet and author

Comparison: The biggest worries

BIGGEST worries. Having left the paid work-world the top worries are:

1. Unforeseen emergency situations that may impact me personally or financially. *A top worry for all.*
2. My personal health and that of my family. *The pandemic has amplified concern for personal health of family and friends.*
3. Losing personal and professional relationships.

It might seem odd that finances are not in the top worries for women who have left the paid work-world. Women out-of-the-paid-work-world have figured out their finances before leaving work or shortly thereafter; thus, finances are not a major concern. It's interesting to see that finances are a BIG worry for professional women in the thick-of-it and working on my-own-terms, ranking number-one for both.

Not a worry. At the very bottom of the worry list are items that may still be on the radar with a bit of uneasiness, but they are not of primary concern. Women out-of-the-paid-work-world are <u>not</u> worried about:

- Safety. *Living in a safe environment with choices as they age. Bottom of all the lists.*
- Needing to move, leaving friends and/or family. *Bottom of all the lists.*
- Financial plan to be 100 years old, that will provide sustainable support. *This ranks near the top for women in the thick-of-it (#4) and those on their-own-terms (#3).*

I worry about...	Out of paid work-world ⬇	Thick-of-it	My-own-terms
Unforeseen emergency	★★★1★★★	★★2★★	★★2★★
Health	★★2★★	5	7
Professional Relationships	★3★	7	6
Health insurance	4	6	5
Being bored	5	★3★	4
Finances	6	★★★1★★★	★★★1★★★
Place to live	7	👎8👎	👎8👎
Safety	👎8👎	👎👎9👎👎	👎👎9👎👎
Need to move	👎👎9👎👎	👎👎👎10👎👎👎	👎👎👎10👎👎👎
Financial Plan to be 100	👎👎👎10👎👎👎	4	★3★

The table above shows the stack rankings in comparison to women out-of-the-paid-work-world. Look at how different the three work groups are. 1=High★★★ and 10=Low👎👎👎

Concerns. Somewhere in the middle of the worry list for women out-of-the-paid-work-world, are concerns of:

4. Health insurance coverage or healthcare choices. *High on the mid-stack for all. A lot of the worry is because*

there are so many things that we can't control in the healthcare system, government oversight and insurance.

5. Being bored with not enough to do. *Mid-stack for all.*

6. Financial means to maintain their current lifestyle. *This is number-one for women in the thick-of-it and on my-own-terms. It takes time and energy to figure out the finances but women out-of-the-paid-work-world have managed it.*

7. Place to live that is affordable and meets their needs over time. *Low on the mid-stack for all.*

Family, health, and finances

Family relationships. Leaving the paid work-world allows professional women to connect with family in a new way. We asked them to think about family relationships (considering their immediate family: spouse/partner, children, parents, and siblings).

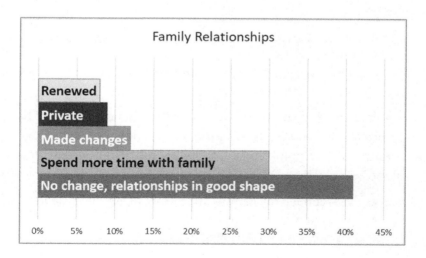

249

- 8% revived and renewed family relationships.
- 9% told us this was a "private matter" and to mind our own business.
- 12% made changes in some relationships and "set some things straight".
- 30% spend more time with family members.
- 41% didn't change anything, maintaining their good family relationships.

Age. In our survey, the average age of those who out-of-the-paid-work-world is 67.

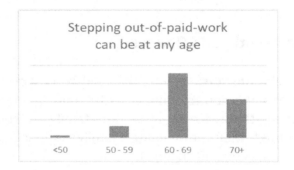

- 2% are younger than 50.
- 9% are between 50 and 59.
- 56% are between 60 and 69.
- 33% are age 70 or better, which is the largest number of respondents this age group.

Health. Leaving the paid work-world opens opportunity to improve health. We asked survey respondents to consider health as a combination of exercise, nutrition, stress, and sleep.

- 48% "upped my game", improving their general health.
- 43% maintained their level of health.
- 7% experienced declining health.

Health

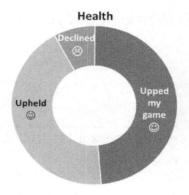

Finances. Professional women out-of-the-paid-work-world generally view their financial position as stable. Financial stability may take a bit of adjustment and time to figure out, as we learned in *Chapter 7: A Curiosity*.

To determine their financial position, we asked respondents to consider a combination of pension (work or government), savings, and how many years they expected to live.

- 57% are very confident, comfortable, and secure.
- 34% are reasonably good and on track.
- 7% are probably okay, but are not entirely sure.
- 2% are worried and concerned.

Financial Position

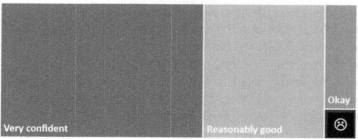

Appendix 2: Worksheets for What the Heck to Do Now

CORE VALUES (CV)
set the foundation

What fundamental principles (standards, ethics, etc.) define you?
E.g., authenticity, compassion, dependability, kindness, fearlessness, honesty, loyalty, optimism, pragmatism, etc.

What causes or basic rights do you believe in?
>> Reflect on the Gross National Happiness questions in Chapter 4: Happiness, Wellness, and Healthcare, especially questions 1, 3, 7, 8, and 9.
>> Consider others, such as animal rights, charity, community development, death with dignity, education, environment, equality, historic preservation, religion, support for the arts, etc.

People you admire. How? Why?
From history, work, play, reading, family, etc.
Who are they? What do they represent, for you?

PERSONAL INVESTIGATION (PI)
tunes into the unique life you lead

Answers to your own key questions.

- *Are you satisfied with where you are?*
- *What risks are there to making a change?*
- *What flexibility do you want?*
- *What are you most worried about?*
- *Are you living the life of your hopes & dreams?*
- *What would you do if you could not fail?*
- *What are you most grateful for?*
- *Are you proud of who you are? Why/why not?*

THE SEVEN W-H QUESTIONS
expand your PI

Who, What, Where, When, Why, How, and How Much?

- **Effort**: *Full-time, part-time, no-time (when and how much)?*

- **Substance**: *Type of work and the contribution (what and why)?*

- **Engagement**: *Self-employed or employed by others (who and where)?*

- **Composition**: *Structure versus flexibility (how and where)?*

WELLNESS QUESTIONS
examine multiple dimensions

- **Physical:** *Are you satisfied with your current physical health (exercise, nutrition, sleep, etc)?*

- **Mental:** *What is your engagement with the world through learning, creativity, and social awareness?*

- **Emotional:** *How open are you to empathize and accept others?*

- **Spiritual:** *How does spirituality factor in your holistic search for meaning and purpose?*

- **Social:** *What importance do you place on connecting and interacting with people?*

- **Environmental:** *What role do you play in supporting a positive environment, locally or on a larger scale?*

DEVELOPMENT PLAN (DP) inspires action		
Objective	**Action/Resources**	**Your Goals**
Get or Keep Current	• *Workshop(s)* • *Online course(s)* • *Self-study*	
Expand Expertise	• *Books* • *Research ... what?* • *Find a mentor/coach*	
Continued Education	• *Attend lectures* • *University programs* • *Expand contacts* • *Vocational programs*	
Related Experience	• *New things to pursue* • *Volunteer opportunities* • *Intern, shadow*	
Other...	• Board Appointments	

CV + PI + DP = IAP

| Core Values | + | Personal Investigation | + | Development Plan | = | Intersection of Activity & Purpose |

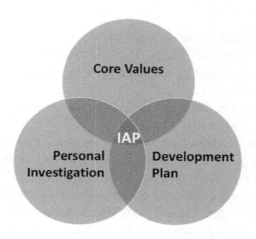

Core Values

IAP

Personal Investigation

Development Plan

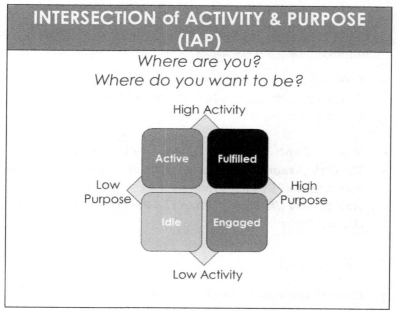

INTERSECTION of ACTIVITY & PURPOSE (IAP)

Where are you?
Where do you want to be?

High Activity

Active

Fulfilled

Low Purpose

High Purpose

Idle

Engaged

Low Activity

Appendix 3: References and Resources

BOOKS

Includes thick-of-it insights

- **Achieve with Grace:** *A guide to elegance and effectiveness in intense workplaces* by Theresa Lambert
- **Grit – The Power of Passion and Perseverance** by Angela Duckworth
- **Leading from the Edge:** *Global Executives Share Stories for Success* by Annmarie Neal
- **Resilience: It's Not About Bouncing Back:** *How Leaders and their Organizations can Build Resilience Before Disruption Hits* by Jennifer Eggers and Cynthia Barlow
- **Workquake:** *Embracing the Aftershocks of Covid-19 to Create a Better Model of Working* by Steve Cadigan
- **Your Tool Kit for Success:** *The Professional Woman's Guide for Progressing to the C-Suite* by Dr. Sheila A. Robinson

Includes on my-own-terms insights

- **Encore Career Handbook:** *How to Make a Living and a Difference in the Second Half of Life* by Marci Alboher
- **Lean In:** *Women, Work and the Will to Lead* by Sheryl Sandberg
- **Now It's Clear:** *The Career You Own* by Jane Horan
- **The Eighty-Year Rule:** *What Would You Regret Not Doing in Your Lifetime?* By Claire Yeung
- **Your Second Life Begins When You Realize You Only Have One** by Raphaëlle Giordano

Includes out-of-the-paid-work-world insights

- **Encore:** *A Journal of the Eightieth Year* by May Sarton

- **Empty Nest, Empty Desk, What's Next?** *How Boomer Professional Women are Reinventing Their Retirement* by Dr. Rita Smith
- **The Power Years:** *A User's Guide to the Rest of Your Life* by Ken Dychtwald, PhD & Daniel Kadlec

Includes financial insights

- **Charles Schwab Guide to Finances After Fifty** by Carrie Schwab-Pomerantz
- **Your Money or Your Life** by Vicki Robin and Joe Dominguez

Includes wellness insights

- **Authentic Happiness** by Martin E. P. Seligman, PhD
- **Becoming** by Michelle Obama
- **Bouncing Back**: *Rewiring Your Brain for Maximum Resilience & Well-being* by Linda Graham, MFT
- **Designing Your Life:** *How to Build a Well-lived, Joyful Life* by Bill Burnett & Dave Evans
- **Hector and the Search for Happiness** by François Lelord
- **Threescore and More:** *Applying the Assets of Maturity, Wisdom, and Experience for Personal and Professional Success* by Alan Weiss, PhD
- **You Look Good for Your Age,** *An Anthology* edited by Rona Altrows

Other insightful books

- **Adoption Detective:** *Memoir of an Adopted Child* by Judith Land
- **My Own Words** by Ruth Bader Ginsberg

WEBSITES

- www.adultdevelopmentstudy.org
  A Harvard Medical School and Massachusetts General Hospital 2nd generation study on Adult Development.
- https://advertising.expedia.com/
  Expedia Media Solutions
- https://www.gbta.org/
  Global Business Travel Association
- www.globalwellnessinstitute.org
  The Global Wellness Institute's mission is to empower wellness worldwide by educating the public and private sectors about preventative health and wellness.
- www.nationalwellness.org
  The National Institute of Wellness provides professional development and engagement opportunities promoting whole-person wellness.
- http://www.oecd.org/
  Organization for Economic Development
- www.plant-based4health.com
  Empowering you to build and maintain a healthy immune system – naturally.
- www.RemoteYear.com
  Keep your job. See the World. RemoteYear.com curates community-based travel programs, enabling people to live, work, and grow in inspiring locations.
- www.SoulHealingStudio.com
  A Sanctuary for Healing and Spiritual Transformation.
- www.who.int
  The World Health Organization works worldwide to promote health, keep the world safe, and serve the vulnerable.

ARTICLES

- *5 Tips for the Millions of Singles Heading into Retirement Solo*
  - https://www.forbes.com/sites/davidrae/2019/05/21/retirement-solo/?sh=618829355319
- *Health Insurance Affordability Concerns and Healthcare Avoidance Among U.S. Adults Approaching Retirement*
  - https://jamanetwork.com/journals/jamanetworkopen/fullarticle/2760437
- *Judging Health Systems: Focusing on What Matters*
  - https://blogs.sph.harvard.edu/ashish-jha/2017/09/18/judging-health-systems-focusing-on-what-matters/
- *Just How Bad is Business Travel for Your Health?*
  - https://hbr.org/2018/05/just-how-bad-is-business-travel-for-your-health-heres-the-data
- *What Kind of Happiness do People Value Most*
  - https://hbr.org/2018/11/what-kind-of-happiness-do-people-value-most
- *Many in the U.S. worry about affording healthcare in retirement*
  - https://www.reuters.com/article/us-health-insurance-retirement-idINKBN2042FA
- *CIBC poll finds more than half of Canadian women say financial security contributes to their happiness*
  - http://cibc.mediaroom.com/2020-02-24-CIBC-poll-finds-more-than-half-of-Canadian-women-say-financial-security-contributes-to-their-happiness
- *Women are more financially stressed than men — Here's how to overcome it*
  - https://www.nbcnews.com/know-your-value/feature/women-are-more-financially-stressed-men-here-s-how-overcome-ncna1055901

Appendix 4: Timeless Questions

We are all shaped by our personal history, our family, and those who have gone before. Writing this book, we reconnected with how our parents shaped their relationship with the work-world, and we want to introduce you to them.

Janet's mother, Dorothy Farwell Anderson, was a graduate of George Washington University. She was an active stay-at-home mom while the three kids were young. She volunteered at the school, as a Cub Scout Den Mother, and gave sewing lessons in the inner city of Chicago. Once the kids were out of the house, she went on to get her master's degree and became a reading specialist.

Janet's father, Alton Dewitt "Andy" Anderson, was also a GWU graduate, which is where he met Dorothy. He was a physicist and engineer working in the early days of the space program. He was actively involved with the National PTA (Parent Teachers Association) and an avid golfer. He holds patents for applied engineering of laser technology. The later years of his career were spent working with the U.S. Department of the Navy.

Janice's mother, Josefine Maria Weisgerber, grew up in a small town in the region of Alsace located in northeastern France on the Rhine River plain. Bordering Germany and Switzerland, it has alternated between German and French control over the centuries and reflects a mix of those cultures.

Josephine's early years as a teenager found her squarely in the midst of World War II. She narrowly escaped death, lost a beloved family member, and her brother disappeared, never to be heard from again in her lifetime. Her passion to survive, take new risks by leaving her country, and find a new career path in Canada shaped her core values of compassion, kindness, honesty, and fearlessness.

Janice's father, Theodor Arnold Schneider, was Swiss. Josefine and Theodor immigrated to Canada in the early 1950s. They built their new life together in Canada, although neither spoke English or French when they first arrived. In the early years, Josefine worked in many trades supporting the family. Theodor was a structural engineer, specializing in the construction of hydroelectric plants throughout eastern Canada.

An archeological dig

When news reports of COVID-19 first turned to shelter-in-place guidelines, the calendar was cleared and Janet's attention turned to cleaning and reorganizing a storage room in the house. It was like an archaeological dig peering into boxes that had not been opened since she moved ten years earlier. Some were labeled and others were not. Surprisingly, some labels even matched the contents.

Among the artifacts Janet came across were three overstuffed file folders, each bursting and spilling out. The file folders were yellow with age. The contents were surprising: in 1985 Janet's mother Dorothy and a friend embarked on a survey to write a book about retirement. The parallels to what we were doing was astounding.

The contents of two folders were newspaper and magazine clippings of topical articles and humor from a time before the internet, cell phones, portable GPS, hybrid cars, and Google. One folder contained typewritten documents on larger-than-life legal-size paper, 8.5" x 14", hanging three inches out of their folder to reveal neat yet uneven characters, typed on a manual typewriter with a ribbon.

Janet recalled memories of the family dining room with neat stacks of papers and a modern but manual typewriter. We chuckled at stories of pens, paper, and machinery magically disappearing for dinner parties and holidays, only to reappear the following day as if never disturbed.

We had fun reviewing the contents of those folders. The news and magazine clippings all dated from 1985 to 1987. It was a thirty-five-year-old snapshot in time revealing how much times had changed and, remarkably, how much they hadn't.

Dissolving the boundaries

Digging into these written artifacts we discovered that Dorothy and her friend were looking for answers to questions about what came next. We were also looking for answers to similar questions ... thirty-five years later.

Both of us used a survey to gather information. Their survey was printed and distributed via snail-mail while ours was conducted electronically using SurveyMonkey, email, and social media. Both surveys posed closed- and open-questions to gather statistics and stories. We recovered more than sixty of their surveys. In our electronic age, we were able to collect more than 650 survey responses.

The parallels of human transition were undeniable.

The joy of travel hasn't changed. Travel is and was the number-one desired activity when not working. The 1985 survey asked additional insightful questions. More than half traveled worldwide (54%), about one-third traveled only in North America, and the rest (13%) kept travel close to home. Each trip was for longer periods of time than we expected.

| 14% >1 month | 35% travel 3-4 weeks at a time | 41% keep trips to 1-2 weeks | 11% A few days |

In Dorothy's survey, time spent with family and friends was most treasured. Only 17% spent holidays quietly or alone, while 82% always celebrated with family and friends.

A number of people (22%) continued to work part-time or explored a new career, working in nursing, the library, the school system, business consulting, or as a board member.

Then as now, many of our great worries never materialize. Finances and boredom are two top worries before leaving the work-world. This is identical in both the surveys, with finances being top of the list for both. In both time periods, these great concerns didn't develop into the expected problems. We suspect that the simple act of worrying about something allows us to address and solve it.

Some things haven't changed between the 1980s and the 2000s. We still complain about the high cost of medical care and prescription drugs.

In both surveys, 40% of the respondents chose to remain anonymous (41% in Dorothy's survey and 38% in ours).

Revealed truths

In the 1985 survey, more than 65% reported that they were working to simplify their life.

- ❧ Putting fewer things on the calendar.
- ❧ Getting rid of stuff.
- ❧ No wasted time commuting.
- ❧ Things can wait.
- ❧ Take it one day at a time.
- ❧ Sleeping in.
- ❧ Less scheduled.
- ❧ Staying _out_ of activities.

That sounds too familiar. These are similar strategies to those described by women out-of-the-paid-work-world in *Chapter 7: A Curiosity*.

Our survey was directed only to professional women. Dorothy's survey was directed to both men and women professionals, with survey responses from 67% females, 27% male, and 6% combined responses.

The good news is that in the mid-1980s, 81% considered their health to be good and that improved, rising to 92% in our 2019 survey.

An unexpected number was that 35% of Dorothy's respondents reported they were widowed and 95% of those were women. Statistically the average lifespan for both men and women has risen. We are living longer healthier lives today.

Year	Female	Male
1980	77	70
2020	81	76

The result was 58% in a committed relationship with 42% single in the 1980's survey, as compared to 78% in a committed relationship in our survey, with 22% single.

It was interesting to see involvement in unique activities.

- *New hobbies and interests*: clowning, ham radio, canning, stained glass, writing, and sculpture – as well as more expected activities like caring for grandkids, attending book clubs, and going to the gym.

- *Interesting volunteer work*: hospice, bloodmobile, tutoring, neighborhood patrol, and meals-on-wheels.
- *Further education*: communication skills, investments, financial planning, and learning to map old land grants.

Dorothy asked for strategies to jog the memory, a quarter simply said they didn't have any, but more than half offered advice. Here are the top four suggestions:

1. Notes to self.
2. Keep a calendar.
3. Concentrate and don't get distracted.
4. Give it time ... go to sleep and the answer will come to you at 3:30AM.

Wisdom through time

Two questions in Dorothy's survey asked for "advice and suggestions" or "adages and quotations." Nearly everyone provided a response. Here are a few of our favorites:

Advice:

- ➷ Prepare for an all-new lifestyle.
- ➷ Be yourself! Live it up! Do it!
- ➷ Do things that are fun, develop new skills, learn something new each day.
- ➷ Love what you are doing, plan and set goals.
- ➷ Don't lose your sense of humor. You will need it.
- ➷ Don't worry about things like money or work; they will work themselves out.
- ➷ Look around, there are thousands of things to do.

Quotes:

- "Don't look back. Something might be gaining on you!" — Satchel Paige, professional baseball pitcher.
- "If you think only of yourself, the road is long and the load is heavy. It's not the load that breaks you down; it's the way you carry it." — Lena Horne, American singer, actress, civil rights activist.
- "It ain't over until the fat lady sings." — An old colloquialism or proverb inspired by the opera.
- "Procrastination is the thief of time." — Edward Young, English poet and philosopher.
- "Remember the past, plan for the future, but live for today, because yesterday is gone and tomorrow may never come." — Saint Luke, one of the four Biblical Evangelists.
- "When I hear somebody sigh, 'Life is hard,' I am always tempted to ask: Compared to what?" — Sydney J. Harris, journalist and author.

Reflection

What a delight to get a snapshot in time. We can see that these are timeless questions that span the generations.

We embarked on this two-plus-year project to write a book. Dorothy collaborated with Fran Hayes on their book for two years from 1985 to 1987. We both used surveys for a research foundation for our books. We published our book in 2021. Sadly, Dorothy and Fran never did finish their book.

We don't really know why Dorothy and Fran's book went unfinished. Janet suspects that it was because her brother

Bob died in the summer of 1987 and that turned life upside down for the whole family.

In Dorothy's file folders we found this delightful card. It was designed and painted in June 1985 by Joyce Anderson, Bob's wife; she is proud and happy to share it with you.

In letters accompanying the survey, Dorothy described her project as wanting to be "a jokey book." So, we leave you with a photo of a few clippings found in that old yellowed folder.

These clippings did not have accompanying dates or source information. Signatures on some of the jokes, cartoons, and quips reveal the talented and thoughtful humorists.

Tom Armstrong
B. Brown – published in the Wall Street Journal
Dik Browne (1917-1989)
Franklin Folger (1919-1977)
Ann Landers (Eppie Lederer 1918-2002)
Joseph Mirachi (1920-1991)
Rev. Paul Osumi (1905-1996)
Harley L. Schwadron (Schwadroncartoons.com)
James Stevenson (1929 – 2017)
Bob Thaves (1924-2006)
James Unger (1937-2012)

NOTES

Made in United States
North Haven, CT
30 November 2021